THE COLLECTED POEMS OF
WILLIFFE CUNLIAM
EDITED BY SIMON RENNIE

KFS
Newton-le-Willows

Published in the United Kingdom in 2024
by The Knives Forks And Spoons Press,
51 Pipit Avenue,
Newton-le-Willows,
Merseyside,
WA12 9RG.

ISBN 978-1-916590-02-1

Acknowledgements:

Although it is beyond the scope of this volume to detail their contributions,
and with sincere apologies for any omissions, in a variety of ways the following
people and organisations have helped make this collection possible:

Arts and Humanities Research Council, Shirley Ashton, Kirstie Blair, Burnley
Central Library, Malcolm Chase, Dea Shaw, University of Exeter, Exeter Centre
for Victorian Studies, Faustus, John Goodridge, Brian Hollingworth, Karin
Koehler, Brian Maidment, Ruth Mather, Francis O'Gorman, Rob Spence, Mike
Sanders, Gregory Tate, Libby Tempest, Charlotte Tupman, *Journal of Victorian
Culture*, and Edward Walton.

In addition, special thanks are due to those who generously contributed to the
Go Fund Me campaign to assist in the costs of the production of this collection.

Two people whose contributions should be briefly described are: my publisher,
Alec Newman, whose enthusiasm for this project takes me back to our
discussions about northern working-class Victorian poetry when we first
met almost twenty years ago; and my partner, Rachel Jardine, whose support
throughout has ranged from encouragement to collaboration, with the
resurrection of 'Sweetheart Fair' from a barely legible smudge being largely
down to her genius.

Contents

Introduction   vii

A Wedding Rhyme ...   1

Labor Omnia Vincit   2

Praying George   3

Adieu!   5

Sweetheart Fair   6

Weighing the Anchor   8

Th' Petched Shirt   10

Strike While the Iron is Hot   12

Hoamly Chat   13

Vanitas!   15

Congratulation   17

Misgivings!   18

The Daisy   19

Settling th' War   20

God Help the Poor   22

Thenkful Jone   24

The Little Star Gazer   25

'Sham Abrum'   26

Love!   28

Come Bob, We've tu Markit i'th' Taon   29

Despondency   31

Work, Lads, and Think   32

Sundey 'T Moarning   33

Granny!   35

Owd Jinny's Egsperianze   36

Frost-Work (as 'Williffe Cunliffe')   37

Our Darling (as 'Williffe Cunliffe')   38

A Humble Tale   39

Hora Fugit!   41

A Rhyme for the Time   42

The Lass o' Pennul Waytur   43

The Angel of My Home   44

Guilty, My Lord!   45

Heaven!   46

'Leather-Yed Tay'   47

Not for Ourselves Alone   48

Nellie's Grave   49

The Evening Bell   52

The Sabbath Bells   54

The Passing Bell   56

Spring Time   58

The Stolen Bud   59

Sunshine   61

Little Billy   64

Inscription   66

Poesy and Poverty   67

'Aor Peggy's Courting!'   70

Sleep   71

Maud Mary   72

The Recluse   73

Benediction!   75

Home Longings   76

Tear-Drops   77

The Glance of Love   79

Notes   81

THE COLLECTED POEMS OF
WILLIFFE CUNLIAM
EDITED BY SIMON RENNIE

Introduction

Professor Simon Rennie, University of Exeter

'Williffe Cunliam' is the pen name of the blacksmith William Cunliffe (1833-1894), who published poetry in the *Burnley Free Press and General Advertiser* (later the *Burnley Gazette*) between 1863 and 1866. As far as is currently known, Cunliffe was not published anywhere else, so the fifty-four poems contained in this collection represent all of his known output. Considering that there was a gap of almost two years before his last two poems appeared in the paper, this body of work was produced in a very short space of time, if indeed the poems did not exist before they were published. For about eighteen months, at the height of the Lancashire Cotton Famine of 1861-65, 'Williffe Cunliam' was effectively the 'house poet' of his local newspaper. In the mid-Victorian period it was not unusual for manual workers to have their work published in local newspapers, and most publications regularly included poetry columns offering one or more pieces written by local contributors. This obviously provided free copy for the newspapers, but these columns were also sites of entertainment, aesthetic appreciation, social and political comment, and reportage. Reading Victorian local newspaper poetry is a good way of gauging what ordinary people thought about the world around them, but also what they *felt*. This is particularly important when examining the devastating social effects of the Cotton Famine.

The Lancashire Cotton Famine was largely caused by the Union blockade of Southern Confederate cotton exports during the American Civil War of 1861-65. This had catastrophic consequences for the northwest of England, where the economy was almost entirely based on cotton production, with its raw material mostly sourced from the American South. At the time there were more than two thousand cotton mills in the region employing almost half a million people. The Cotton Famine led to unprecedented levels of unemployment and reduced working hours, which in turn led to widespread poverty and hunger. When I began looking at poetry related to the Lancashire Cotton Famine in 2015, I first researched the *Burnley Free Press and General Advertiser* holdings at Burnley Central Library, and it was Williffe Cunliam's work that I first read. What immediately struck me was the quality of the verse I was reading. The dialect poetry alone was extraordinarily rich in its variety, but also clearly served to preserve local speech patterns, and to provide astute social observation and commentary. On a basic level, it was just very engaging and entertaining work. I can remember laughing out loud at 'Settling th' War' ('chaps wi' noddles full o' larning') in the library reading room – no-one told me to 'shush'. I quickly realised that here was a Lancashire dialect poet at least as fine as Rochdale's Edwin Waugh, Blackburn's William Billington, or Ashton's Samuel Laycock, who had remained undiscovered in the archives for 150 years. Later that year I was employed by the University of Exeter as a lecturer and in 2017 I was lucky enough to secure a substantial grant from the Arts and Humanities Research Council to recover and create a database of Cotton Famine poetry. That database now contains 398 poems by scores of different poets on the subject of the worst economic crisis to afflict the region, but Williffe Cunliam's work still stands out as an extraordinary testament to the wit and skill of working people's engagement with literature in the nineteenth century. Far beyond the few poems of his contained on the database, this collection shows the full breadth of his talent, including a wide range of topics and styles covered by his 'standard English' poetry.

Almost everything we know about William Cunliffe's life confounds expectations we may have had about working-class northern English industrial life. There were two 'William Cunliffe's' living in Blackburn during the Cotton Famine – one a blacksmith, and one a wool sorter. It was partly one of his own poems which helped to identify our Cunliffe as a blacksmith. 'Th' Petched Shirt' begins with the line 'One day, reight anenst aor smithy ... ', with 'smithy' indicating a blacksmith's workplace. Very soon further research corroborated this, and it was clear that the writer of the poems was this working-class metal worker. However, although Cunliffe's economic fortunes rose and fell during his lifetime, his father owned a large farrier and wheelwright yard in the Pickup Croft area of Burnley, so he was not an impoverished labourer. William Cunliffe was in fact a skilled manual worker, and his poetry indicates a good level of education, whether this was institutional or self-taught. He also had much broader life experience than we might expect of a Lancastrian manual worker. In 1853, at the age of twenty, he sailed to New Jersey from Liverpool on the Roscius and spent the next five years living in the United States. Little is known of his time in America, but it did inform his attitude to the political implications of the American Civil War. Living back in Burnley during the conflict, he was a vociferous opponent of potential British intervention in the war, believing that the existing British policy of neutrality was for the best. Contemporary newspaper reports place him at political meetings across the region, arguing against those who thought Britain should side with the Union in the later stages of the conflict. While this counters the myth of wholesale Lancashire working-class support for the Union, it is interesting that this political stance is not reflected in his poetry. When it touches on the subject of the American Civil War Cunliffe's poetry is observational and politically even-handed (see 'Settling th' War', 'Hoamly Chat', or 'Thenkful Jone').

After the war, and the Cotton Famine, Cunliffe married Mary Hargreaves, a farmer's daughter from Habergham Eaves, and they had a son, William, in 1871. Also in 1871, the census reveals that he was an employer of fourteen men. However, the business partnership he had formed to become a manufacturer of ironwork gates and palisades soon got into trouble and he was declared bankrupt in 1873. He subsequently moved with his family to Deptford, London, where he was first employed as an engineering draughtsman and then as a civil and mechanical engineer. He died of heart disease at his home, 33 Harcourt

Road, Deptford, on 25 February 1894. More details of Cunliffe's life can be found in his entry for the *Oxford Dictionary of National Biography*. The main reason why this working-class writer has an entry in the *ODNB* is because of the attention his work received when the Lancashire Cotton Famine poetry project was launched. Excerpts from Cunliffe's poetry have appeared in the *Guardian*, the *Times, the Sunday Times*, and many other publications, and recitations have been performed on BBC radio several times. It has taken more than a century-and-a-half, but this fine Lancashire poet is finally being celebrated for the quality of his clever, witty, and affecting poetry.

Given that all of Cunliffe's output was effectively published in one newspaper (The *Free Press* became the *Gazette* in 1864), it made sense to present the poems in the order in which they originally appeared. This gives an idea of how Burnley residents would have received the poetry every week – the paper was published on a Saturday – and of how regular Cunliffe's appearances in the newspaper were for well over a year. Of the fifty-four poems collected here, fourteen are written in the Burnley variant of Lancashire dialect. Unlike some of his contemporary vernacular poets, Cunliffe's phonetic spelling of dialect words and local pronunciations is very consistent. While the idea of authenticity in dialect poetry is difficult to determine, the fact that he did not belong to a particular 'school' of poets might indicate that his ear for local speech patterns was relatively accurate, and that we are being privileged with an aural snapshot of Burnley in the 1860s. But, however fascinating the dialect work is, this should not detract from the quality of Cunliffe's 'standard English' poetry. The formal and topical range presented here is quite extraordinary, given the compressed timespan of publication. There are poems on role of art in society ('Poetry and Poesy'), sea shanties ('Weighing the Anchor'), narrative poems ('Nellie's Grave'), gothic tales ('The Recluse') and deeply metaphorical works ('The Stolen Bud'). In terms of poetic form, Cunliffe seems to have been determined not to repeat himself, using a wide variety of registers, diction, line lengths, rhyme schemes, and indentation systems. If we take this alongside the allusions to other writers in his work, it becomes clear that, like all good poets, Cunliffe remained a student of poetry. We could, and should, appreciate his poetry for itself, but it also works as a kind of survey of mid-Victorian poetic range, including a much truer representation of the reality of nineteenth-century social class than would be achievable by more mainstream poets. The poems of 'Williffe Cunliam' lay undiscovered for a century-and-a-half. Now is the time for them to be explored and enjoyed.

A Wedding Rhyme
(For the Marriage-day of H.R.H. the Prince of Wales)

Burnley Free Press and General Advertiser, March 7th 1863

Ring, ring! let glad bells swing
Their peals from a thousand towers;
Shout, shout! let joy ring out
From these happy hearts of ours;
Booming guns across the seas;
Penons streaming to the breeze;
From bow and stern to high top-trees;
   Proclaim our joy to-day.
Speed the joy o'er ocean wide;
Hail the day with loyal pride,
Where'er British hearts abide
    Or own 'old England' sway.

Spread, spread, high overhead,
The flag of the Danish line;
Bind, bind, with flower-wreaths bind
It fast to our royal ensign.
Chiming bells and cheering voice
Welcome, England's royal choice:
Hail the bride with hearty voice,
   And merrily ringing bells.
Banish toil and care away;
Joyous hearts be ours to-day –
On this merry wedding-day,
    Of our lov'd Prince Wales.

Bright, bright, let the glowing light,
Make day of the ev'ning gloom,
Shine, shine, in flame entwine
Devices bright to illume.
May long live the Royal pair,
Mutual happiness to share;
(Waft to heaven our loyal prayer
   Ye joy-betiding gales.)
Bless the husband and the wife;
Stainless – cloudless be their life;
Hearts unmarr'd by cares or strife:
    'God bless the Prince of Wales.'

Williffe Cunliam

Labor Omnia Vincit

Burnley Free Press and General Advertiser, March 29th 1863

Courage! man! be up and doing;
  Seize the moments as they glide;
  Undismayed the right pursuing,
    Ere the darker days betide.

Persevere! be not faint-hearted,
    Though dense clouds above thee loom;
  Be not, in thy purpose, thwarted!
    Brighter moments, too, will come.

By stern trial undeterred be;
    Make each circumstance thine own:
  And more resolutely gird thee
    For the task, if Fortune frown!

Let not wind and tide, man, drift thee
    Listless, in the adverse gale;
  From thy cold indifference lift thee;
    Ply the oar, and bend the sail!

Difficulties will beset thee: –
    Mould them with an iron will
  To thy purposes, and get thee
    Good from ev'ry passing ill.

Trifle not! place no reliance
    In the flatterer's tempting tongue:
  Struggle on, and hurl defiance
    To each obstacle! – be strong!

Trust in God! when darkness lowers;
    Duty's path, unswerving tread.
  Noble deeds, like fragrant flowers,
    Wreath thy memory when dead.

Praying George

Burnley Free Press and General Advertiser, April 4th 1863

Aot fra' the dingy smoky taon,
   Aw offen like tu stray,
  Un catch God's free, refeshin' air,
    Upon the Sabbuth day.

Un oft aw've met un oddish chap
   Seengin' reight lustily,
  O' quaint un ranting good owd hymn,
    Tu quarest melody:

'Twer praying George, o' good mon,
   Wi' pious, simple haort;
  Whoa az o' coyler raond the taon
    Won'st ues't tu trail his cart.

But naoh, o' poor owd scavingcr,
   He sweeps the mucky streets;
  Un trails the nast and durt away,
    Tu arn the breod he eights.

Yo'd meet him wi' o' weel-worn hat,
   Quite rusty, on his yed,
  O' threed-bare coyt upon his back,
    Ut gin him sum one hed.

Stout fushten breeches on his legs,
   Un big clogs on his feet,
  Come clomping – honds beheend his back –
    Seengin' wi' all his meeght!

O' chap wonce ax'd him, wheer he's baon?
   Just when he'd stop't tu blow.
  Wi' pleasing smile, the good mon said,
    'Aw'm baon to heaven, arn't yo?'

He seys he's baon to trail abaot
   Yon cart a few weeks more,
  Un, then, he's baon to be a king,
    His wark un troubles o'er.

Ut vary soon he'll swap his rags,
    Fer blood-wesh'd roabs of leet;
  Then happy live for iver-more,
    Un reign i' glory breet.

He's knelt him daon be't lone road-side,
    Whell tears, like patterin' rain,
  Fell fra' his cheeks, un towd the Lord,
    'He's sinful, praud, and vain.'

'Aye, George,' aw thought, if thah art praud,
    Such hoamly duds¹ drest in,
  Thee i' th' clogs, owd hat, un coyt,
    Wote'er mun aw heh bin?'

'T would touch yer haort tu see him pray,
    Knelt o' the green gerse sod;
  Un yer the good owd cratur, there,
    Paur aot his soul to God.

Aw think we all mud summat larn
    Fra this good, gradely soul;
  Un live contented wi' aur lots,
    Un dunnot grunt and growl.

Theer's mony a one ut's weel to do,
    Un niver wants a meel,
  Ut hezant hoaf soa good o' haort,
    Un duzent thankful feel.

---

¹ clothes

Adieu!

Burnley Free Press and General Advertiser, May 30th 1863

Bound over the ocean – over the ocean,
    Unto a far land across the rough sea,
  Still feeling for thee a lover's devotion,
    Dearly lov'd England, I wander from thee.

The meadow, the greenwood, the garden, and orchard;
    The scenes of young days I mentally see,
  And memories dearer – the graves in the churchyard
    Where lie the dead forms that are sacred to me.

The bustling town with its smoke-wreaths upcurling,
    From tall taper-chimneys upreared by each mill;
  The clatter and din of machinery whirling,
    Gave music and pleasure that's sweet to me still.

Will this affection – this patriot-passion,
    Ever grow cold when afar off stray?
  Will these emotions e'er have a cessation
    When over the ocean away – far away?

Over my eye-sight the dewy mist gathers;
    Feelings of sadness upon my heart prey;
  Oh, my dear home-land! – old home of my fathers!
    Shall I ever forget thee? – O never! nay, nay.

When in my distant rude cabin I ponder,
    And pictures of 'olden time' pass in review,
  Then shall love for the old land grow fonder,
    And flowers o'er the pathway of memory strew.

Should foemen assail thee, the children that rally
    To strike for the homes of their fathers a blow,
  Around the old island, from plain, hill, and valley,
    Will send terror's chill to the heart of the foe.

Then farewell my country! and God ever gird thee,
    Around with his presence, from want and from war!
  Dear name! – at the sound my heart ever stirred be;
    And my prayer for thy weal ascend from afar.

Williffe Cunliam

Sweetheart Fair

Burnley Free Press and General Advertiser, June 6th 1863

Up th' New Road, like bees o' swarming, –
    I' ther Sunday cloas soa breet,
  Gay young lads and lasses – charming –
    Strut by scores ut Sunday neet.

Soon uz th' parson leaves off preytching,
    Ur uz t' last 'amen' yo yer,
  Then – sich bustle, un sich streytching,
    Fer tu get aot furst to th' dur.

Maid un mon, fra' church un chapel,
    Make for th' fair thersels tu show;
  Arm i' arm sum bowdly grapple,
    Others connut sport o' beau.

Un like butterfleas ther flirting,
    Good un bad o' iv'ry shade;
  All ther thowts full bent o' courting,
    Grave and gay o' iv'ry grade.

Un they flutter, flirt, un wriggle,
    Fra' th' Bull nook, tu Roberts-row:
  Stare un chatter, smirk un giggle,
    Just to get o' chap, yo know.

Bonnits stuck all ow'r wi' posies –
    Ribbons yellow, red, and blue –
  Setting aot sum cheeks like rosies,
    Others o' deoth's ashen hue.

Silks, cottons, un merinoes,
    Just like mushroom tops aot-spread,
  Sum, az ugly as e'er seen, pass
    Praudly tossing up their yeds.

Swaggering, arm i' arm soa clever,
    Swells goa, sucking cigar stumps,
  I' paper collars, shiny beavers,
    Peg-top breeches, patent pumps.

Ogling, wi' such airs, the lasses,
   (Tho' we know it's all o' sham),
Thinking iv'ry one ut passes,
   . Is ower yed i' love wi' em.

Fair un foul, leet yed un leet heart,
   Goa there, hoaping soon to pair
Off wi' sum poor love-lorn sweetheart,
   Ut they'll meet ut 'sweetheart fair.'

Williffe Cunliam

Weighing the Anchor

Burnley Free Press and General Advertiser, June 13th 1863

Come, man the capstan quick!
Let us hear its lively click;
Now weigh the anchor, slick,
   Heave, oh, heave!
Push around, my hearty men!
We must put to sea again;
So heave, my lads! amain:
   Heave, oh, heave!
Once more from port outbound –
Aye! – briskly drive her round;
Now – now, she leaves the ground; –
   Heave, oh, heave!
We shall soon be under way;
And, then, gliding down the bay,
O'er the seas away – away!
   Heave, oh, heave!
We must loose each close reef'd sail,
For to catch the fav'ring gale,
Ere its friendly breath doth fail,
   Heave, oh, heave!
Home and land will fade from sight
Ere creep on the shades of night;
But, the sea is our delight!
   Heave, oh, heave!
Though dear friends we leave behind: –
Hearts loving, true, and kind,
Cheer up, boys! – never mind!
   Heave, oh, heave!
For the ones, so dear, we hold,
We will win bright yellow gold:
Like mariners true and bold.
   Heave, oh, heave!
We've a captain good and brave;
And as staunch a barque, we have,
As ever stemm'd a wave.
   Heave, oh, heave!

So come weather fair or foul; –
Come storm, or calm, or squall,
We'll be staunch at duty's call.
        Heave, oh, heave!
We'll cheerily brave the sea;
God speed us! – and, it please,
Heaven to send a fav'ring breeze.
        Heave, oh, heave!

Th' Petched Shirt

Burnley Free Press and General Advertiser, June 20th 1863

One day, reight anenst aor smithy, –
    T'other side o'th' wattergate,
  Hung sum cloas: – "Well! said Jone, "si'thi,
    Yon's well-petched, at ony rate."

(Theer un owd petch'd shirt wur dangling,
    Flopping clumsily o'th' line,)
  "Aw shud want yon petches mangling
    Daon a bit if yon wur mine."

"Mending ollus shows a sloven,
    Bi th' big petches cloated o'er,
  Wheer it happens to be roven
    Summot like a big barn door.

Steod o' wi' ther sizzers cutting
    Aot wheere'er it's bad un thin,
  Un a gradely bit theer putting,
    Just as if 'twor woven in."

"But," said Jone, "naoh, mending's saving;
    Wives ut cannot mend and darn,
  Si'thi, lad, ur not worth heving! –
    Un ther's sum tu praod tu larn.

Weel-petch'd things ur noa disgraces;
    Poor men's wives mun darn and mend;
  Petches uz just like the plaisters
    Ut they call the "Poor Man's Friend."

Un o' wife ut's good ut stitching,
    Keeps owd cloas boath good un smart;
  Un o' lass ut's 'shamed o' petching
    Hezent got a gradely haort.

Better, far, than I' debt running,
    Weor o suit of petched cloas,
  Better that, than chaps cum dunning,
    Poking bills before thi' nose."

"Well," aw said, "Jone, th'art a nailer,
    Yet, aw welly think th'art reight:
Better mend than gi' tu th' tailor
    Brass ut ow't to goa fur meight."

Williffe Cunliam

Strike While the Iron is Hot

Burnley Free Press and General Advertiser, July 4th 1863

Strike while the iron's hot,
  In its bright glow,
Easy to beat and bend;
  Be not too slow!
Strike while the iron's hot;
  Now is the time –
Forge well thy actions, man,
  Make them 'sublime.'

Strike while the iron's hot;
  Welding each chance
Fast to thy fortunes, man,
  Good to enhance.
Work with a sturdy will –
  Slack not the strife –
Fashion something of use
  For future life.

Strike while the iron's hot,
  Though grime and sweat
Blacken and soil thy brow,
  Ne'er give up yet;
Though sparks around thee fly,
  Ne'er have a care;
And, though thy efforts fail,
  Never despair.

Strike while the iron's hot,
  Ere thou art old,
Soon Death will stretch thy form,
  Stiff 'neath the mould.
Make, shape, while time is ripe,
  Deeds that will last –
Actions that will endure
  When life is past.

Hoamly Chat

Burnley Free Press and General Advertiser, July 11th 1863

"Aw say, des tu yer theer, heigh! Tum,
    Just stop fur a miunit or too;
  Is t' woife, un all t' bairns weel, ut whoam;
    Un aoh gets tu on wi' owd Sue?"

"Wha! weighving ull hardly meight find;
    Aw wish all t' Surat wur i'th pop,
  Foaks seyn, ut if things dunnot mend
    Aur maisters ull soon hev tu stop.

Un cotton, they seyn, 's getting dar',
    Un sich stuff it is, railly,
  It's all through this 'Merikay war;
    Aw wunther wot th'end on it ull be."

"Aye! ut aor haose we hennot ainr'd salt,
    Eight childer, un Dick, un mysel;
  Aw'st caper abaot like o' cault,
    If aw nobbut yeard t' factory bell."

Summot like thirty weeks they'n bin stopt,
    Un nobbut hoalf-time afore hed,
  Aor brass wur soon done, un things popt,
    Fur we hed tu do summot for bread.

Un Dick, when he couldent get wark,
    Sum urn dree, un daon-hearted did look;
  We'd sit theer, baot fire, un th' dark,
    All shiv'ring un huddled I'th' nook.

Un aw've cried to see th' childer baot meight,
    Un cloas, till my e'en couldent see;
  Un aw thought, though I didm't think reight,
    Foaks ud leove uz tu starve un to dee.

But, aye, when they brought the relief,
    Un gie'd uz o' shilling 'o yed,
  Aw thought it aboon all belief,
    Wi' two bran, span, new blankets fur th' bed.

Aor owd cloas wur fettled un petch'd,
    Till they wouldent petch up ony more,
  When they coom, un then fresh uns wur fetched;
    God bless em fur helping the poor.

Naoh, Dick looks as slick as o' snig,
    They've drest him so weel – top tu toey,
  They've gin him o' second-hand rig;
    Un us foine uz a fiddler is Joey.

Awm soa fain, aw mun oat wi 't un tell;
    Un mi haort, sithee, Tum, 's in sich glee,
  Aw hardly can hold wi myself –
    God bless em! – whoaever they be."

Vanitas!

Burnley Free Press and General Advertiser, August 1st 1863

The world's in search of happiness;
   In this continual round
  All men, both fools and sages, press, –
    How rarely is it found!

Each by an 'ignis-fatuus' led,
    Runs on with frenzied haste,
  'Mid pitfills, bogs, and dangers, dread,
    Bewildered in a waste.

As when the alchemists of old
    Sought mystic arts, to bring
  Some power whose touch could change to gold
    A base and worthless thing;

So, each, the baser things of earth
    Seeks out with eager mind;
  But never joys of sterling worth
    Among its baubles find!

An ardent boy, – I longed to clasp
    The moth upon the wing, –
  The weary chase, found in my grasp
    A crush'd and shapeless thing;

So, seeking pleasure, I, since then,
    Have roam'd the wide world o'er;
  But disappointed hopes, and pain
    I gain'd, and nothing more!

I sought it in a poet's pen,
    With all a poet's zeal;
  And flowery poesy, again,
    Did fruitless task reveal!

I sought it in the wondrous page
    Of scientific lore –
  Studied philosopher and sage,
    But vainly did explore.

My heart grew sick of luring joys,
　　That withered at the touch –
Of phantom hopes, and vain decoys;
　　Why care or live for such.

The heart was but an aching void,
　　Longing for something more –
Some purer joy – joy unalloyed,
　　Unrotten at its core.

At last I turned my thoughts to God,
　　In penitence and prayer,
Confess'd the sinful path I'd trod,
　　And sought forgiveness there.

In broken accents of despair
　　I prayed to be forgiven;
For grace to turn from worldly care,
　　And look to God and heaven.

And then I found that purer joy,
　　And inward sense of bliss,
That peace which death cannot destroy,
　　That long sought happiness.

Congratulation

Burnley Free Press and General Advertiser, August 1st 1863

Joy betide thee! – joy betide thee!
   Blessings rich and rare be thine,
  Heaven guard thee! Heaven guide thee!
   Best and brightest hours be thine.

He, who to the altar led thee –
   Pledged his life and love for thine –
  May he, from the hour he wed thee,
   Happy make that heart of thine.

Peace and plentiness surround thee;
   Sweet domestic bliss be thine;
  Every grace and virtue 'round thee
   And thy fire-side circle, shine!

And when future years shall steer thee,
   Near the shadowy close of life,
  Hope still cheer thee! angels bear thee
   To still happier spheres of life.

Williffe Cunliam

Misgivings!

Burnley Free Press and General Advertiser, 8th August 1863

Wilt thou forget me, when far off I wander, –
   When I, alone and disconsolate, stray?
  Or say, will thy heart on our intercourse ponder,
    And thy thoughts cling to him who is far, far away.

Will this fond passion prove transient and fleeting,
   As light as the breath of a close summer's eve?
  Shall heart to heart in warm response beating,
    Beat but to torture, to mock, and deceive?

Are there no ties to bind our hearts closer,
   Which time, space, or changes can never destroy?
  Shall false regard e'er make the bond looser,
    Or to the true heart prove a wanton decoy?

Nay, I'll not blame thee, though frail some may deem thee, –
   Though weak were thy friendship, 'tis but like the world,
  To judge thee so harshly, would but ill beseem me;
    A passion toss'd waif on life's eddy whirled!

"'Tis the way of the world,' – though loud its profession,
   How feeble its practice, – its friendship – how stale!
  The heart that loves truly, meets but with derision;
    And friendship's a virtue deem'd foolish and frail.

The Daisy

Burnley Free Press and General Advertiser, August 15th 1863

Meek little daisy in hedgerow and lane,
Welcome! sweet flower, in spring-time again,
Peering, obscurely, amongst the rank weeds;
Or silverly, spangling the green, grassy meads.
Welcome! sweet daisy, – companion of spring –
Welcome the memories thou to us doth bring.

Dear – dear mementoes! ye bring in your train
Thoughts that are mingled with sweetness and pain.
Thoughts of the 'olden times' – thoughts that I love,
Of days when gay garlands of wild flowers I wove;
Of bright boyish hopes – of bright golden hours: –
Things that have withered, as ye must, fair flowers.

Hast thou, sweet daisy, no lesson to give? –
Yes! – thou canst teach me, like humbly to live,
By life's dusty roadside, or, cold, rugged slope,
My mission, fair flower, like thy petals, to ope';
On ditch-side or meadow as sweetly to grow
And in sunshine or shade, shed life's beauties below.

In white and gold, crimson tipp'd dress, I ween
Ye are fit flowers for adorning a queen!
And the crimson-stained crest reminds me that blood
Has made pure the souls of the sainted good –
Thy golden corona, and brilliant white,
Of their shining crowns, and robes of light!

Williffe Cunliam

Settling th' War

Burnley Free Press and General Advertiser, August 22nd 1863

Wot's the matter? – wot's the matter? –
 Wot's theas folks, all staning raond?
Hez ther sum'uddy bin feightin,
 Ur ther's sum'uddy kill'd ur draown'd?

Oh! aw know, naoh, – aw'd forgettun –
 Welly six-months, fur ur nar,
Heer aor parlyment's bin meetin,
 Bizzy settling o' th' war.

Chaps wi' noddles full o' larninng;
 Yeds ut's brasting wi' ther wit,
Heer yo'll find, boath neet un morning,
 Gie'ing the world the benefit.

One owd mon, seys "it's noa wundther
 That all t' roagues, ut's goan fra heer;
You, should get tu differin, feightin;
 That's no'at natteral, un clear."

"It's theas steom looms," seys another,
 "Cotton for th' hond-loos ut whoam,
Wi' full time, we've hed tu last uz
 For a hunther'd yeors tu cum.

Un, bi weighving upo' th' hond-looms,
 We'd a hed anuff tu dun:
'Cause this steom-loom stuff's like cobwebs;
 'T weors aot – ten tu hond-wove one."

Un another, seys, "theas haythen
 Ar'ent larn'd like gradely foaks,
Un they're awful wicked craturs, –
 That yo know, ut reads I' books. –

"Furriners, kicking up ther rumpus,
 Mony a time we'n hed tu lick;
Un theas 'Merikuns weont bi quiet,
 Till John Bull goas wi' a stick."

Soa they argy, tone geon tother, –
   Baon tu hev it, right ur wrong,
  Till yo'd a 'most think they'd at it
    Wi' ther neohves, uz weel uz't tongue:

This mon threopin, all for Davis,
   T'other Lincoln, fair ur faol, –
  Tongs un poker, whang, bang at it,
    Spit un sputter, gern un graowl.

Well! chaps, hurry up the bizness,
   (Let's hoap th' end on't's getting nar)
  Spout away at Nuttall's corner,
    Finish th' job, un settle th' war.

Williffe Cunliam

God Help the Poor

Burnley Free Press and General Advertiser, August 29th 1863

God help the poor! who, day by day,
  The woes of want do feel;
Whose hardest toil, in brighter hours,
  But earned a scanty meal;
Who, hapless, lag, with hungry looks,
  And cheeks, so gaunt and pale,
That tell, so mutely eloquent,
  The starvling's piteous tale.

God help the poor! – ye rich and high,
  With lands and mansions fine,
Think of the poor in their cold, bare homes,
  Can you let them starve and pine?
Think of their shivering rag-clad limbs,
  And spare, from your plenteous board,
A crust, for to fill their foodless mouths;
  A mite from your golden hoard.

God help the poor! from hunger's pangs,
  In their dark hours of need;
Thy providence supplies their wants,
  And better days, God speed!
And brothers, ye with bursting purse,
  Give from your plenteous store;
In deeds of noblest charity,
  Give – lend to your brother, the poor!

God help the poor! let better days
  Dawn on our suff'ring land;
Let men in unity and peace,
  Clasp firm the friendly hand,
And brothers greet, with honest hearts,
  Of high and low degree,
And all men join – a happy band –
  In blissful amity.

God send us peace! let discord, war,
    And men's dissensions cease;
Oh! give to mourning millions
    The blessed boon of peace!
Let brothers sheath the cruel sword –
    Fierce battles ended be;
Let foes be friends! And man to man
    Breathe love and charity.

Williffe Cunliam

Thenkful Jone

Burnley Free Press and General Advertiser, September 5th 1863

Bless God for a dinner!
Tho' aor porridge gets thinner,
Tho' aor meel be a clemm'd un, un meight we heh noan,
Thank God for it allus,
If He thinks tu doal us
But prators un salt, 'baot o' bit uv o' boan.

Tho' poor un hoaf clemmin,
Un scraping and skeamin,
Tu keep just alive, un get summot to eet;
Let's try to make merry –
Feel thankful and cheery,
It'll breetun aor troubles, un make 'em seem leet.

Ther's nout con distress us,
Wi' o' good haort tu bless us,
Dry porridge ull e'en taste as good as roest beef;
Un, baot beef or pudding,
We'll feost like a good un,
O'th' bacon and peyse, ut we geet fra' th'relief.

Un, when th' war is settl'd,
Un foughten, un battl'd,
Till peohce comes agean, tu show ut aw'm fain,
Aw'll 'luminate th' winder,
O' penny sho'nt hinder,
Aw'll stick aw few tallow-dips up agean th' pane.

Un then, when possessing
Full wark, un its blessings,
Aw hoap ut aw sho'nt get aboon wi' mysel;
Content as God pleases,
Wi' just wot He gi'es us,
Let's be thankful, humble, un bide wi' His will.

Un, if we are starving,
It's what we're deserving,
It's all o' His goodness we're lettun tu live:
His marcy's unstinted –
Aor lives angel-tented;
Let's thenk Him, un bless Him, for wot He does give.

The Little Star Gazer

Burnley Free Press and General Advertiser, September 12th 1863

Little one, little one, with the bright eyes
 Gazing so wond'ringly up at the skies,
 Hast thou learnt to love too, the clear starry night? –
  Are they not pretty – those great orbs of light?

Dost thou think that those stars are driven in there,
 Like the bright-headed nails in thy grandpapa's chair –
 With glittering heads of a silvery white,
  And studding the throne of the great God light?

Or deemest them holes in the curtain of sky,
 That veileth yon heaven from faint human eye,
 Where glimpses of heaven's bright glory are seen,
  Brighter than burnished gold or silver sheen ?

Or think'st thou like daisies amid a green field –
 Those sparkling stars on their dark azure shield –
 And – wert thou a bird, thou wouldst fly up, away,
  And amongst the bright flowers of yon bright heaven play?

Little one, tell me, who think'st thou could strew
 Those jewels of light o'er the heavenly blue?
 Who, tell me, but God climb th' ethereal height,
  And hang up those lamps in the great dome of night?

Or, perhaps, thou tell me thy thoughts little one,
 Thou dost think of some lov'd little playmate now gone,
 And wonder if thou, like thy playmate, must die,
  And dwell a sweet angel beyond that fair sky.

But little one, little one, fret not, nor sigh,
 God will take thee to heaven, if good, bye and bye;
 And a circlet of stars, bright as those, thou shalt wear
  On thy brow when an angel; – then little one, cheer!

Williffe Cunliam

'Sham Abrum'

Burnley Free Press and General Advertiser, September 26th 1863

Wot puff, un talk, gert ado,
They meyn when big foaks deen!
But owre o poor un common chap
Foaks winnot wet ther e'en:
We see 'em one day walking th' streets,
Un th' varry next ther goan;
Un few beyon ther oan harth-stoans
Abaot ther berrin knoan.

Aw met o' chum, but t'other dey,
He sed, 'Sham Abrum's deod;'
It seem'd just like o'thunner clap
Cum mashin throo' mi heod!
'Sham Abrum! nay, wot will ta say?
Goan deod? aw knew him, weel!
Deor aot![1] aw think hiz poor laom wife
Mun feoful badly feel.'

Tu chapel ur tu church, noa moar,
Hur wheelin cheer he'll thrutch;
Noah shu, agean, wi' warkin haort,
Mun stump it wi' hur crutch.
Un az hu seez hiz big clogs stond
Unused bi th' chimley nook,
Hu'll sit, un freot, un cry, aloan,
Ut Deoth hur Abrum took.

He couldn't boest o'brass ur geer:
A rough, ungainly mon,
Donn'd up i' petch'd, mud-plaster'd cloyse,
He waddl'd, goping on;
Noah bewty marks were on his face,
His yare like brissels stood,
But tu hiz poor, laom, limpin' wife,
He wer allus kind un good.

---

[1] dear heart

Throo' dust un deet – throo' mire and weet,
He's swept the streets o'th' taon,
But Deoth coom wi' hiz besom too,
Un Abrum laid hiz doan:
For Deoth hez got a besom, big,
Un wi' it, off he sweeps
Both gert and small, good, bad, un all,
Tu th' church-yard deod dust heops.

Williffe Cunliam

Love!

Burnley Free Press and General Advertiser, October 3rd 1863

Love they say is like a vapour,
　　Like a fitful shower in May;
Like a flickering wasting taper, –
　　Flame and spark will pass away.

Love is fickle, ever-changing,
　　And inconstant, so they say,
Now a fierce tornado raging,
　　Now a languid zephyr's play.

But pure love is true and lasting,
　　Earnest, trusting, come what will –
Summer's scorching – winter's blasting –
　　Pure love liveth, trusteth still.

Woe or weal our hearts be nearest,
　　Friends may fail, and friendship wane,
But in night – the darkest, drearest –
　　True love's star will brightest reign.

Death the fondest ties may sever,
　　Heart from heart be torn away,
Yet true love will live for ever,
　　Life nor death shall break its sway.

Earthly joys oft scorch and sear us;
　　Living souls here part in pain;
But one precious hope can cheer us –
　　Hearts in heaven will meet again.

Come Bob, We've tu Markit i'th' Taon

Burnley Free Press and General Advertiser, October 17th 1863

'Come, Bob, we've tu markit i'th' taon,
    Aw want shuger, un tay, un sum meight;
      Ther's sum brass to be woarn, for it's Sunday tu-morn,
        Un ther's now't mich i'th' haose fur tu eight.'

'Get off wi thi! – goa bi thisel;
    Mon aw allas bi petticoyt-led –
      Un goa trailing wi thee for the shuger un tay,
        Aw bin tee'd enuf sin aw wer wed!'

'Nay! Bobby, naoh, dunnot say soa!
    Wha – thah knoaws thah't o' cumfurt to me.
      Tho aw feel rayther hurt, bless thi! luv is noa foart:
        Un aw'll niver say sich wurds to thee.

Thah knoaws when a lass i' mi' teens –
    When o' coortin thah coom iv'ry neet,
      Thah sed when aw wer goan, thah felt seckless and loan,
        But soa comfurtsome when aw'r i'th' seet.

Thah knows haoh thah foller'd me round;
    Feyther couldent o' lick't thi awey,
      Thah mony o' time, sed iv aw'd nobbut be wed,
        Thah'd do just az aw'd want, neet un dey.

I'th dark it's o' leng, loanly gait;
    Un it's dreesome 'baot thee when it's leet.
      If thah stops heer ut whoam, happen sumuddy'll come,
        Un thah'll goa un get druffen tu-neet.

Aw've tu buy thi sum stuff for new sherts;
    Un aw've don on o' clen, tidy gaon;
      We con call ut owd Mat's for a pipe and a chat –
        Heer's thi hat un thi coyt – come, aw'm baon.'

'Aw'll goa lass; aw knoaw aw've done wrang,
    Aw desarve o good claot abaot th' yed;
      Hardly wakken'd ur wick, aw'r as crabb'd as a stick,
        Ur aw'd never o' soa to thi sed.

Bless thi, lass, thah'rt o fortin – thah art!
    Fur thah's' somehaoh sich kind, winning ways,
  O chap connot think ill, let him du wot he will,
    When he looks o' thi bony, breet face.'

Despondency

Burnley Free Press and General Advertiser, October 24th 1863

Troubled, troubled, restless, tossing,
    Like the waves upon the shore:
Fears and doubts, the sense engrossing,
    Hang, the gloomy conscience, o'er.

Thoughts that seem like doleful warnings;
    Terrors vague, beyond control.
Spring up strange unwonted yearnings, –
    Undefined, within the soul.

Cares, like cankering acids, eating
    Deep into the tortur'd heart; –
Writhing, groaning, vainly beating
    Pleasure round to lull its smart.

To the heart, the past life sendeth
    Back no single ray of cheer;
And the future no hope lendeth,
    All o'ercast with clouds of fear.

Oh! to rest the lab'ring spirit;
    Oh! – the troubled heart to calm;
Oh! were but the pangs that stir it
    Lull'd and sooth'd by Gilead's balm.

Williffe Cunliam

Work, Lads, and Think

Burnley Free Press and General Advertiser, November 7th 1863

Rise to the task with good heart in the morning,
  Seek not, the duty of labour to shirk,
 Labour degrading? the thought rightly scorning,
   Willingly, cheerfully bend to the work.

Not like a thing, without meaning or notion,
  Wielding the hammer with dull senseless clink;
 Not a machine, with but one line of motion,
   In round unvarying, – work, lads, and think.

Think of the men who have laboured before you;
  Think of the brave hearts that laurels have won;
 Not stooping like cravens, hard lot to deplore you –
   The race is half won if in earnest begun.

Look – look around on the triumphs of labour,
  Think of the blessings 't has brought, nor then shrink
 From hope in the task; with aim in your labour,
   Honestly, earnestly, work, lads, and think.

Nor with ambition for fame or for station;
  Seeking applause from the popular tongue,
 Though praise may be from the heart of a nation,
   Rightfully, truthfully, honestly wrung.

What, though your worth by the world unconceded?
  With good honest toil your fortunes still link:
 Toil bringeth blessings – obscure and unheeded;
   Work for the love of it, work, lads, and think.

Sundey 'T Moarning

Burnley Free Press and General Advertiser November, 21st 1863

'Twer Sunday't morn, just eight o' th' clock,
　　When t' wife t' last childt wur bizzy donning;
Un wesht un drest, donn'd i' ther best
　　All t'other raond bi' th' table stonning
Wi faces breet, soa pleosed un sweet;
　　(Like weel rubbed apples – red un shiny)
Un th' spoons un th' porridge bowls set aot;
　　Soa breet, they shoan like raol chiny.

Th' haose floar wur cleyn – weel sanded o'er
　　Un th' weel scaur'd harstoan white az t' ceiling
Th' top bar unth' oon, wi' th' things aboon,
　　O'th jaumstoan, like o'bran new shilling.
Cheers, drawers, un th' kist, – clock case un th' rest
　　Like lookin'-glasses fairly glitter'd:
Polish't soa breet, ut th' blazing leet
　　O'th' fire upon 'em donce't un flitter'd.

Un theer stood Tum, o'th' table side,
　　O'mecking butter-cakes, quite bizzy;
Wi' th' kettle on, un th' porridge pon,
　　Un th' watter in em, hot un fizzy,
Wi' roll't up sleeves, his horny kneaves,
　　Grabb't hold't o'th thible wi o' florridge,
Then dabb't into th' meyl-pot like o' mon, –
　　Un went to th' mecking childer's porridge.

Un wi' the steom o' merry tune,
　　Humm't aot fra' th' throyht o'th copper kettle,
Un whel he thumpt, the porridge jumpt,
　　Un donce't, like wick things fu' o' mettle;
Un th' childer's een wur sparkling seen,
　　As Tum gie'd th' mess extra stirrage,
Then topple't aot i'th' biggest dish
　　O' rare, hot, smooking mess o' porridge.

Un watchin' wisht as mice they be,
  Whel' Tum to aich o' share iz messing,
Then, cloasing han's un een they stan',
  Whel' upo' th' meel he seys o' blessin',
Un aot o' th seet soon th' porridge geet,
  Whel' spoons i'th' bowls med lively clatter,
Then soon daon th' street o'th roayd to th' school,
  Wi' leetsome haorts their feet did patter.

Granny!

Burnley Free Press and General Advertiser, December 5th 1863

Since days of my childhood, ah! years have passed – many;
   Its friends are all changed and a many are gone,
  But one there was true, then – my dear, good, old granny,
   I'm sure that she lov'd me if no other one.

I can picture her still – no memory sweeter –
   The snowy-starch'd cap, that hugged her face close,
  With its big scallop'd frill, and each time-honour'd feature,
   And the old-fashioned 'specs' set a-straddle her nose.

I think I can see her now, – darning a stocking,
   While from the big Bible a chapter I read;
  Then she'd pat me, and praise me, her chair gently rocking;
   But I lov'd best her cakes, and her nice gingerbread.

Poor Granny! – how painful at last was our parting;
   When verging on manhood, the years grew apace,
  And your boy said 'good bye!' for a foreign land starting,
   How the tears roll'd down your sorrowful face.

As I held your old hand, and with tears tried to cheer you,
   'In a year or two, Granny, I shall recross the main,'
  But her broken voice said, 'When you go, ah! I fear you
   Will ne'er on earth meet your Granny again.'

Williffe Cunliam

Owd Jinny's Egsperianze

Burnley Free Press and General Advertiser, December 12th 1863

Aw've lived i' this world, naoh, yers turned o' fourscore,
    Un fea'ful gurt changes i' moh toime aw've sin,
  But things upon airth meck the haort sick and saur,
    Un th' best things abaot it's but bother and din.

This hub-bubble life, wi' its sweets turning saur,
    (Through an owd woman's spectacles see't az aw've sin;)
  Uz like bad stuff to tek wi' sugar yep'd ower,
    Wi' o' good deol o' sin, pride, un meck-believe in't.

Aw've sin foaks grow rich ut wur varry poor;
    Fra' th' top o' th' lather sum tumble in th'ditch;
  Un ut last beg ther breod fra' door-hole to door.
    Soa fortune! life's weigh-scales does up and down twitch.

Aw've sin sum meck brass fly like dry dust abroad;
    Going spreeting abaot i' feshion's fine togs; –
  But uz poor uz o' crow, at last, werking i'th' road,
    O raggle't stoan-breyker, i' gurt, iron clogs.

Young wenches, soa hoapful un gay i' ther teens,
    Aw've sin to rags, hungher, un druffeness wed,
  Un sum erring craters, once howty uz queens,
    I'th' warkhaose dee, rueing the yure off their yeds.

Egh! haort-wracking tales hez un owd woman yerd;
    Un haort-wracking seets has an owd woman sin:
  Seets soa dreffle – to meck th' haort's-blood turn to curd –
    Haorts broken, hoaps brasted, lives wasted i' sin.

Awm tired o' sich sight seets, un my owd frien's are goan,
    They've topple'd i'th' grave, aot o' seet one by one;
  Aw're ower-lived my time, un awm freoting aloan;
    This life, like owd Joab, aw'd not allus live on.

Aw'd fain rest theos owd warking boans under t'sod,
    This weary owd yed i' the shraod fowds aw'd lap;
  Aw'm langing to dee; – if it nobbut pleased God,
    This world for o' better aw'd willingly swap.

Frost-Work (as 'Williffe Cunliffe')

Burnley Free Press and General Advertiser, December 19th 1863

All over the window –
   All-over each pane,
  Unseen ringer traceth
    Beautiful shapes again;

Filigree-work of silver,
   Sparkling in the light;
  Delicate devices,
    Fashioned in the night:

Richly chased in silver.
   Scroll-work, leaves, and flowers,
  Cascades, cliffs, and castles,
    Facades, domes, and towers,

Landscapes, brightly glowing;
   Scenes from fairy-land;
  Miniatures of Heaven;
    Wrought by Master-hand!

Ever-varied patterns,
   Wondrous – chase and fair –
  Into loveliest fabrics,
    Interwoven there: –

Quaint and queer, yet lovely,
   In many a rare design,
  Bright, adornments glisten,
    Crystal wonders shine.

Man's most gifted pencil –
   Cunning workman's skill,
  Not a pane could ever,
    With such fancies fill.

God-life wonders! – teaching
   That Omniscient Mind
  All the works of nature,
    Governs, and designed.

Williffe Cunliam

Our Darling (as 'Williffe Cunliffe')

Burnley Free Press and General Advertiser, January 9th 1864

Two laughing eyes, that are sparkling and bright,
　　Happy and innocent, joyous and light –
　Undimmed by sorrow – unting'd by care,
　　Young love and tenderness outglancing there.

Two pretty cheeks that with rosiness glow,
　　Much-treasured curls that in soft clusters flow;
　Two cherry-lips that are waiting a kiss,
　　With a coy, smiling face that is radiant with bliss.

Two little pet feet, ever tripping in play,
　　Actively pacing her child-life away;
　Two little hands, that never are still,
　　But busy – obeying her capricious will.

And a sweet syren voice, like clear silver bell,
　　Breaking the silence of sweet sylvan dell;
　Blithely carolling like love-bird in bower,
　　Is like a bee, humming from flower-bell, to flower.

Now, it is baby-house, set out in play;
　　Now, dressing dolly in colours more gay;
　School-marm, 'tis now, teaching pussy, A, B;
　　Then the grocer, who's weighing out sugar and tea.

Now begging dough for to make a doll-cake;
　　Now, teazing mamma some nice thing to make;
　Now, mamma's dress must be sewn with a pin –
　　Thus in a thousand ways childish arts win.

So be our darling's life – guileless and fair,
　　Unsullied by sin, sorrow, trouble, or care;
　God be her guardian amid dangers rife;
　　Blest be her mission, and happy her life.

A Humble Tale (founded on fact)

Burnley Free Press and General Advertiser, January 16th 1864

Mine is no tale of blood, and soldier's valour,
    Of mighty deeds performed in daring strife,
  Of greatness raised from penury and squalor,
    'Tis but a simple tale of humble life.

Two maiden-sisters lived and loved together, –
    The only tenants of a lowly cot;
  Through shade and shine – through all life's stormy weather,
    They patient toiled, contented with their lot.

Each Sabbath found them in a homely dress,
    (The unpretending garb of decent poor;)
  Amongst her scholars, each within her class,
    Teaching of Him who did the cross endure.

They were poor, yet, cheerful, struggled on,
    And earned their bread by labour at the mill;
  And when God pleased to helpless stretch the one,
    The other toiled, resigned and cheerful still.

Some said, the parish workhouse should provide
    For all her sister's wants; but no, her zeal
  So patient and heroic, at her side,
    Still found her toiling for a scanty meal.

Through years of suffering, trial, want – how long!
    She turned her busy mangle, day by day,
  Sweet'ning her labours by a Christian song,
    As cheerful as a happy child at play.

Long years ere this, one woo'd her for his own,
    She lov'd him, but at duty's stern demand,
  She would not leave her parents, old and lone,
    But, for their sakes, refused a lover's hand.

Oh! deep the grief and pain these tidings gave
    To her true heart, – alone she sat and cried
  Oft o'er his fate, yet cheerfully, though grave,
    She toiled on for her parents till they died.

A palsied sister, now, left to her care,
    Dependent on the gains her mangle brought
(Which often brought to her but meagre fare,
    Though simple wares she sold to eke it out.)

And now the worn-out soldier did return,
    And with warm embrace fell many a tear.
Her heart unselfish – would not from him turn,
    Though sickly and wounded from a Kaffir's spear.

His services a paltry pension gain'd
    Which scarce sufficed to serve his merest need;
But in her cottage, welcome, he remained,
    She only happy all his wants to heed.

With care most anxious every wish would find
    Her by his side as every week wore round,
With cheering words to soothe his fretful mind,
    And tender hands to dress his rankling wounds.

She felt in heart, and Heaven's sight, his bride,
    Wedded in soul, – and soon the rites had blest
Their marriage, – but he shortly sank and died –
    Died in her arms – died, pillowed on her breast.

Trusting in God, whatever should betide,
    Through sorrows deep, unaided and alone,
Till, like her sister struck, she sank and died,
    And in a grave was laid, without a stone.

Hora Fugit!

Burnley Free Press and General Advertiser, January 23rd 1864

Yet to live we are permitted;
    And to greet each friendly face;
Many forms, well-known, have flitted
    From this earth, and done their race.

On they pass in long procession, –
    Friends deceased – in solemn train: –
Whose turn next comes in succession?
    Death will soon be here again!

Death is certain – life uncertain;
    Youth gives no security:
Soon the land will draw the curtain
    Shutting out futurity!

Ev'ry breath is one less given;
    Each pulsation of the heart,
Nearer brings to Hell or Heaven; –
    Soon the silver cord will part! –

Even now the strands are breaking –
    Life holds by a ruptured thread! –
Ev'ry motion's a death-token:
    Soon the grave will be our bed.

Williffe Cunliam

A Rhyme for the Time

Burnley Free Press and General Advertiser, January 30th 1864

Times are very hard, my friends; –
And, still lower trade descends;
But be not despondent, friends,
    After night comes morning!

Luck in life oft downward tends; –
Sweet and bitter with life blends;
Grief makes joy the sweeter, friends:
    Evils good returning!

He who waits and hopes for, friends,
No good fortune e'er attends:
All his dreams in nothing ends,
    And – through life goes mourning.

But, who on himself depends,
Needs not go a-begging friends:
Fortune to him favour lends,
    Honest worth discerning.

Go not trouble-seeking, friends;
Oft the cloud a shower portends;
Day o'ercast in sunshine ends;
    Ev'ry lane's a turning.

Then be not down-hearted, friends,
Let us fit our means to ends;
Keep heart till the future mends;
    Lessons from want learning.

The Lass o' Pennul Waytur

Burnley Gazette, February 6th 1864

Fra' Worsthorn Moor to Whalley Nook,
    Gawthrup, and Pennul waytur,
      There's bonnie flaors for them ut look,
        I' colours true to Naytur.

But poesies breet and sweet may be,
    Wi' mony o' lovely faytur;
      But to mek as ther's noan suits me,
        Like th' lass fra' Pennul waytur.

Aw wish aw'd Taonley's land un brass,
    Aw'd gie' it all to mate her,
      But gowd con't buy yon bonnie lass,
        Ut blooms bi' Pennul waytur.

Hu' hoam wor baon one neet fra' th' taon,
    Soa I went wi' her o' geytur,
      When we'd to part aw left mi' haort
        Wi' t' lass o' Pennul waytur

Aw dunnot care wot foak's may sey,
    Fur love is human naytur;
      Aw dreom bi' neet, aw dreom bi' dey,
        O' th' lass o' Pennul waytur.

It may be wrang to sing o' sang,
    I' praise o' human cratur,
      But love soa strang, mecks daft the tangue,
        Ower th' lass o' Pennul waytur.

Williffe Cunliam

The Angel of My Home

Burnley Gazette, February 13th 1864

A little fire-side angel,
  A heart-engaging child;
So modest, and so beautiful;
  With winning airs, so mild:
A face reflecting all her soul;
  A heart with nought of guile;
God spare thee! angel of my home,
  To cheer my heart awhile!

What – home or life without thee
  And the prattling of thy tongue?
I have gained fresh heart and courage
  From the music of thy song:
When, hard and cold, the heart has grown,
  And from toil, care-worn, I come,
Thou human makes my heart again;
  Sweet angel of my home!

But oft my jealous heart conjures
  A thousand spectral fears:
The joy, that brightens up the eye,
  May be dissolved in tears:
The angel-idol of my home
  May vanish from my sight; –
God grant my dotings may not end
  Like broken dreams at night!

Guilty, My Lord!

Burnley Gazette, February 20th 1864

What am I, Lord, that I should dare
　　To breathe to thee a single prayer? –
　Why should thy blessings throng my way;
　　And fresh joys gladden day by day?

Thy hand screens me in ev'ry storm;
　　'Mid dangers thick shields me from harm.
　With lavish hand my path is strewed
　　With bounties great, and rich, and good.

What am I? – Oh, Great God! so good –
　　An ingrate – thankless, – Lord, I brood
　O'er fancied ills, and self-wrought cares;
　　And mutter selfish, meanless prayers.

Yet, loving God! thou deigns to heed,
　　With gracious care, my every need;
　And gifts most princely dost thou grant;
　　Anticipating ev'ry want!

What am I, that thou God, so great,
　　Should care about me or my fate; –
　Should seek my rebel-heart to move
　　By deeds of grace, and tones of love?

A wretched, sin-stained worm am I
　　Foul in the slime of vice I lie:
　A thing of earth, for vengeance meet,
　　And yet uncrushed beneath thy feet!

Oh! rebel-pitying loving God,
　　Who Calvary's blood-stained path hath trod,
　And hell's own pains bore in my stead,
　　Shed mercy-beams upon my head !

Yes! – mercy, mercy! – spare me Lord, –
　　Strike not with thine avenging sword; –
　No rebel yet e'er asked in vain,
　　Bestow thy pardoning grace again.

Williffe Cunliam

34 Heaven!

Burnley Gazette, February 27th 1864

Bright Heaven! – when scann'd by mental sight –
Like lovely plains in darkest night,
Or landscapes hid in misty haze,
Too dense to yield to human gaze,
Leaves poesy's farthest flights behind –
The wildest fancies of the mind
Leaves like a blank. The farthing light
Is something, by the moon's sun – bright;
But words, and imag'ry, and thought
Are lost; when Heaven-contrasted, naught;
And while amaze the soul doth fill,
We can but lisp 'Bright Heaven!' still.

'Leather-Yed Tay'

Burnley Gazette, March 5th 1864

Jimmy Joyful, – he-wur a reight jovial cur:
   O weyver, good, gradely and gay;
  But they sed in his yed o waik place he hed –
    He'd o liking fur leather-yed tay.

When welly gin aot, and goan up t'spaot,
   Wi' jading an' weyving all t'day,
  To strengthen his legs and put wind in his bags,
    Ther wur nought equalled leather-yed tay.

Un once in a while, ta cleyn aot t'stomach's bile,
   Un wesh away ailments un ills,
  It'll beot whul kegs-ful o'the best kester oil,
    Un big barrows-ful o' 'Parr's Pills.'

Un haoh fine! when neet comes, wi' a few rousing chums,
   To kest wark and owd care awey,
  Un to thaw aot ones haort ow'r o big brimming quart
    O rate stinging leather-yed tay.

Well, he'd just get a glass, he thought, as he'd pass,
   Th' 'Pig and Whistle,' one Setterday neet,
  Soa his stomach he swill'd till top-heavy fill'd
    His noddle, un his pocket get leet.

Wi' a rollicking load, starting for his aboad,
   He hugg'd the owd pump on his way;
  Un ax'd it to 'take, fur owd bygone's sake,
    O wee drop o' leather-yed tay.'

Then he bowster'd his yed in o ditch fur a bed,
   Un snor'd like a donkey ut beay,
  Till o 'bobby' him spied in the black slutchy tide,
    Happy – dreaming of leather-yed tay.

Williffe Cunliam

Not for Ourselves Alone

Burnley Gazette, March 12th 1864

Not to itself, doth the sun keep its light;
  Not for themselves, the stars glitter at night;
Not for itself the tranquillent breeze blows;
  Nor for itself, sheddeth fragrance the rose;

Not for themselves, do the bright blossoms bud,
  Or clustering berries hang in the green wood;
Not for itself, mellow fruit, yields the tree;
  Nor for self, only, stores honey, the bee.

Nor for itself, guggles forth the clear spring;
  Not to themselves do happy birds sing:
All of God's bounties through whomsoe'er given,
  Are common to all – from earth or from heaven.

Earth is made glad by the golden sunlight;
  Stars shed a beauty o'er heaven, at night;
Breeezes kiss off the foul humours of earth;
  And the rose sends its fragrance on gentle winds forth.

The bee finds its honey concealed the bud,
  In the wild berry the bird finds a food;
The tree, to man yieldeth fruits, rich and profuse;
  And the hive yields its treasure of sweets for his use;

Life, health, and beauty, to all, bears the spring;
  And hearts are gladden'd while merry birds sing;
All God's creations, in earth or heaven,
  Are engaged in dispensing the bounties – God-given.

Nor, fretful man! for thyself shouldst thou live,
  Strength, wealth, time, talents – and all God doth give,
Never were given to gloat o'er with greed;
  Thou art God's almoner! – give where the need.

Nellie's Grave

Burnley Gazette, March 19th 1864

Whiling idle moments,
    From the inn, outstraying,
Of a country village,
    Where I then was staying,

From a mass of verdure
    An old steeple towered;
And I found grave-yard
    In a wood embowered,

And that grave old turret,
    From the green wood peeping,
Was the church; it's walls o'er
    Moss and ivy creeping. –

Haunted by the jackdaw,
    Clad in sable plumage;
Mingling its croakings
    With the hymns of homage.

'Twas spot of beauty! –
    There, the chisell'd outline
Of the quaint old stonework
    Hid in rose and woodbine.

And the gray old headstones,
    Of that silent ground,
Wreath'd in flowers and leaf-sprays
    O'er the sacred mound.

But – one grave, marked 'Nellie,'
    Near a grim old yew;
Grass-grown, and untented;
    Where no flower stem grew; –

'Strange!' I thought, and queried, –
    'With it rests some story,
Known unto the sexton,
    Bent with age and hoary.'

So I asked him, briefly,
    Who this Nellie was?
And a touching story
    He related, thus: –

'Nellie was stranger! –
    At the close of day,
In the flowery spring-time,
    Nellie came this way; –

Came from – none knew whither,
    On the rough highroad;
Seeking for a cottage;
    To make her abode.

And at Widow Goodheart's,
    In the village, stayed,
Where, for board and lodging,
    Week by week, she payed.

Young in years – near twenty –
    Glossy golden hair;
Cheeks like paling roses;
    She was wondrous fair!

And so kind and gentle,
    Though she came alone,
Lov'd by all who knew her –
    Lov'd by ev'ry one!

But her mein grew sadder;
    And her cheeks more pale:
As if some deep sorrow
    Mingled with her tale.

Gossips sought her story;
    But, 'twas never learned;
Some thought her an orphan
    On the wide-world turned.

Through the gentle summer,
    Until autumn-tide
Lengthen'd the shadows,
    Nellie pin'd; – then died.

There, beside that graystone,
    Nellie's grave was made;
And a babe, there with her,
    Side by side, is laid.

Not a grievance spake she;
    Not a murmer muttered;
Wrapt in mystic silence,
    All her wrongs unuttered.

Smiled her cheek so pallid,
    But her eyes sad gleaming,
Full of melancholy,
    Gain-say'd all the seeming.'

In her breast close-hidden
    Ev'ry sign of feeling: –
In her tortur'd bosom
    All unrest concealing.

Who can tell the anguish
    In that bosom striving?
Love, in fierce contention,
    Heart asunder riving?

Anguish far too bitter
    For outward unveiling;
Speech, and sigh, and tear-drop
    At their fount congealing.

Williffe Cunliam

The Evening Bell

Burnley Gazette, April 2nd 1864

Sweetly sounds yon chapel bell
   In the ev'ning's stillness;
  Waking chords within the heart –
    Chords that touch and thrill us!

Slowly in the distant east,
   Dusky twilight, gliding,
  Sombre curtain o'er it draws;
    The blue heavens hiding:

Closing o'er the cloudless sky
   Ev'ning's sable drapings;
  While the sun sinks in the west,
    Wrapt in gorgeous trappings.

The sun-monarch's regal robes
   Wake not unmix'd gladness;
  For the mem'ries of the hour
    Mingle joy with sadness.

Panoramas of the past,
   On the deep'ning shadows,
  Skilfully remembrance paints –
    Scenes of where life led us.

Earliest youth to manhood's prime,
   Incidents thick crowding:
  Act on act, with facts most strange!
    Life in romance shrouding.

With the turn of manhood's tide,
   Billowy years fast gather:
  Dashing age-foam on the head,
    Thick in snowy lather.

And, too soon, our lives must sink
   'Neath the rising billows –
  'Neath the tide of time submerged!
    These – the thoughts that thrill us!

Toll on, toll on, chapel bell;
  Wake the soul in sadness!
Bringing back one lucid spell,
  'Mid life's whirling madness.

Let me think, and let me pray, –
  If before – oh! – never,
Ere my soul be call'd away
  To the vast forever!

Williffe Cunliam

The Sabbath Bells

Burnley Gazette, April 9th 1864

Oh! Sabbath bells, – sweet Sabbath bells!
Musically each note swells;
　Re-echoing, echoing,
　　On the breeze;
　Rambling, trembling,
　　'Mongst the trees –
Through the woods, and o'er the vale,
　Bearing forth
　　Upon the earth,
　Now south, now north,
　　The joyful tale
Of salvation's glorious plan –
How the Saviour died for man: –
Ringing forth their tuneful lays;
Swinging forth Jehovah's praise!
　Ringing, singing,
　　On the air: –
　Sounding, bounding,
　　Ev'ry where: –
'Come, O man come, – come to prayer,
　Come, and worship, – come!
Bells are ringing the towers;
Birds are singing in the bowers;
Bees are humming 'mongst the flowers;
　Come, O man come, – come !
　Ev'ry thing is glad to-day;
　Nature wears its best array;
Come, O man ! come – come away,
Come to worship – come!
　Come ye old, and come ye young,
　Listen to Old Wisdom's tongue –
　To the truthful warnings rung;
　Come, – and pray, come, come!
　　Young and gay,
　　Old and grey,
　　Come, and pray,
　　Come, and pray;
　　Come and worship, come!
　　Come ye old, and leave your cares;

Come ye young, avoid life's snares;
Mount your hopes, to higher spheres,
Come to God! oh, come!
  Be it known
  To ev'ry one
  At his throne
  Unwelcome none
Come, then sinner, come!
Come, ye thoughtless, proud, and gay;
Come, vain mortals while ye may;
Come, who will; come, come, – to-day;
Come to God – oh, come!;
Thus proclaims each iron tongue,
While the sonorous chimes are rung,
In ever-varying song,
Floating, – sweet, – away! –
  Swelling gracefully along,
  Sweet, and musical, and strong,
  Rising, falling, softly swung
  On the Sabbath day.

Williffe Cunliam

The Passing Bell

Burnley Gazette, April 16th 1864

The passing bell,
With solemn knell,
Dolefully doth tell,
>   In its deep – deep roll,
>   That another soul
>   Into eternity hath gone:
>   Chaunting in muffled monotone,
>   'Gone! gone!! gone!!!'
All alone,
Hath the spirit flown
>   To the mystic realm, unknown –
>   To the dim and dusky shades
>   Of that ghostly region: – Hades.
It is gone – gone – gone!
To return no more
From the silent world's oblivion. —
>   Never – nevermore!
>   Never spirit that hath entered, –
>   Or that hath unbidden, ventured,
To explore
>   That dark and hidden region,
>   (And they are a mighty legion)
From oblivious Hades shore,
Eer returneth any more.
Loving hearts may rend atwain –
>   Burst asunder in their pain;
>   And the tears well up, and start
>   From the lacerated heart –
>   Hearts in sorrow writhe and groan
>   But, however much they yearn
>   And departed friends bemoan,
Return,
>   When the fleeting life is o'er
They may nevermore!
>   Hark! upon the fitful gusts
>   Echoes of each tolling tone,
There bursts
Ever and anon
>   Strange and weird-like tones!

Now, like wild – unearthly groans;
Now, like ghostly – stifled moans,
Or like startling spirit – wail;
Sobbing, throbbing
On the gale;
As if some unhappy soul
Mingled with the measured toll
Of the mournful bell,
Sounds of horror o'er its fate; –
Prayer remorseful when too late;
Shrieks of anguish o'er its lot
Cries despairing, from that spot
Where hope is ever past!
Moaning, groaning,
O'er the past!
And the sacrilegious blast,
Like a mocking demon, goes
Cachinating o'er the woes –
Howling, laughing, in its glee
O'er a lost soul's misery!
Till chill,
And a thrill,
Fills the human heart with pain;
And, in fear, we hold our breath,
Trembling, at the thought of death,
While the tears unbidden, start,
As we think how soon we part
With the transient things of earth:
With its gaiety and mirth –
And of human littleness. –
How life's pageantries soon pass;
And the body worms consume,
In the gloom
Of the tomb:
Youth and beauty – vain, proud clay
Mould'ring into dust away,
Thus, upon the silence still,
Broke by tones, now deep – now shrill,
As the doleful passing bell
Sounds its solemn – gloomy knell,
Seen to come,
In its boom,
Echoing voices from the tomb.

Williffe Cunliam ·

Spring Time

Burnley Gazette, April 23ʳᵈ 1864

Oh! the merry spring-time comes; –
  Comes with joy in sunny hours;
Comes with fruitfulness in showers;
  Silver clouds are hung on high,
O'er heaven's cerulean dye;
  Smiling floods of golden light
Tingle hearts with new delight;
  And olden hearts are young,
Drinking pleasures newly sprung: –
  Oh! the – merry spring-time comes.

Oh! The merry spring-time-comes –
  Strewing o'er the mead bright flowers,
And sweet vernal buds in bowers;
  And the air with music throngs,
Of the feather'd chorists' songs,
  Gushing forth from copse and glade –
Comes with balm from ev'ry blade;
  And, with song, the rippling stream
Danceth in the sun's bright beam:
  Oh! the merry spring-time comes.

Oh! the merry spring-time comes: –
  Sunshine, in genial flood,
Melts in joy the sluggish blood;
  And the old feel young again;
And the sick forget their pain;
  Careworn cheeks with smiles are bright;
Aching breasts throb with delight;
  Gloomy minds, turn glad and gay;
Children romp and sport in play;
  Oh! the merry spring-time comes.

The Stolen Bud

Burnley Gazette, April 30th 1864

Within life's garden
    Grew a young rose tree;
And on it budded a little bud,
        As sweet as bud could be:
    The empurpled tip
    From its calyx did peep,
            So sweetly, timidly.

At morn and ev'ning,
    Fondling, came the dew;
And it was studded with sparkling gems,
        Of clear and pearly hue;
    Which lovingly press'd
    On its blushing breast,
            Hanging so tremblingly.

Oh, it was lovely,
    The bud to behold,
Lovingly smiled it, dewily
        Mingled with sunshine like gold;
    Like the smiles and tears,
    Like the hopes and fears –
            This fated life to be.

What though the sunshine
    Shone so merrily –
Though the budlet danc'd on the wind,
        So gay and cheerily,
    And the bright sun's rays
    Interthreaded the sprays,
            To gaze at its rare beauty.

There came angel
    To the tree one day
Came – and the sunshine his shadow made cloud,
        Stealing the flower away;
    The dark angel of death,
    Whose cold blasting breath
            Blighted and wither'd the tree.

Off bud was broken:
Spray torn from the heart,
And wav'd the tree sadly and sigh'd,
With its precious bud to part,
'Twas too fair a flower
For an earthly bower, –
Now, it blooms immortally.

Sunshine

Burnley Gazette, May 7th 1864

Bright sunlight –
Golden light!
With soul-enrapt'ring powers.
Whose genial showers
Come after gloomy night,
As heaven's bliss arrear earth's darkest hours.
Shine, summer sun!
In copious showers,
Resplendent, pours
Thy gladd'ning rays
On grass-fring'd ways,
And leafy maze; –
On time scar'd brow,
And vale below;
On waving plains
Of yellow grain,
Whose bosoms surge and swell,
Bowed by the gentle breeze,
As rippling seas
Stirr'd softly by the gale.

Verdant sprays,
Dust-strewn ways,
Buds iridescently bright,
Gladd'ning the sight,
Are gilded by thy rays,
Bath'd in floods of mellifluous light,
O! dazzling sun!
Thy light endowers
Bright golden hours,
And beauteous falls
On dingy walls,
Gray, crumbling halls,
By reed-clad pond:
Or the sun-tann'd,
Storm-beaten thatch –
The weed-grown patch
Is pencil'd by thy light,
As well as bright-hu'd flowers,
And glorious bowers,
Sun-painted and gilt-bright.

My dreamy soul,
   Beneath thy power,
Loos'd earth's control,
   Enrapt doth soar
Above meaner things of toil and care;
   Inhaling fulsome joy –
   With naught of base alloy
    In fulgent blaze;
   And, scanning sense and sound
   The world of speech around,
   Seeks words of potent power;
   But speech seems blank and bare, –
   And words but naked flow,
   Untelling of the glow
     That passion sways
Bounding through every vein!
Fain would I strike the strain
   From my rude lyre –
The spark of heavenly fire
   That glows my soul; –
Fondly the mystic joy impart;
With fire poetic touch each heart,
    Entrancing all.
    But, ah, from heav'n
    It comes, but to the favour'd few
    To whom 'tis given.

Joyous emotions rise,
   Word measureless!
In vain the pen essays
   Them to express:
Language is powerless!

Yet would I give my meed of praise,
   Not as the dark Parsee,
    Bow unto thee:
    A soulless sun.
But to the great Jehovah raise
   My grateful hymn:
   The Sun of suns,
   Whose omnient powers
In ev'ry golden glimmer showers
    Blessings most bright!
   Whose glory on I may not gaze;

As, dazzled by yon bright sun's rays,
Thy attributes, most glorious, daze
　　My feeble sight;
And leaves me speechless in amaze;
　O, Light of lights,
　Weak is my tongue,
　And faint my lays,
To give to Thee Thy meed of praise,
　Thou Benefactor of my days
　Ineffable I feel Thy praise,
　　And end my song.

Williffe Cunliam

Little Billy

Burnley Gazette, May 14th 1864

Little Billy wer his feyther's darling –
  Little Billy wer his daddy's pet;
 On his bonny nob prattily wer curling
   Gowden yure like the breet sunset.

Un daddy tho'ght o' Billy in his weoving,
  Un he sang like linnit at his wark;
 He'd noan o' trooble I' the whole warld grieving,
  He whissel'd, un he chirp'd like o lark.

For he thought 'twer for Billy he wer sleoving –
  To get Billy bread un butter for to eet;
 Un his loom clatter'd music i' its weoving;
  Un his shuttle seem'd to goa more leet.

'Billy, daddy's gooing ho' pennies o airning,
  To buy Billy cloathes, un goodies sweet:'
 Sed his daddy, cussing Billy i'th' morning,
  'Tattah, daddy! come agean at neet.'

Th' cottage winder leet the sunshine throo' i'th' morning,
  When the weover for his weoving hed to start;
 But o curten shut it aot when he'r returning –
  Un it shut aot, too, the sunshine fra his haort.

For the weover fan ut Billy deod wer leeing,
  Cowd un deod – tho' pratty as i' sleep;
 Un his haort, his throyt wer choaking, ut sich seeing,
  Un daon his cheeks the wat'ry floods did creep.

He could'nt speyk, his doating haart wer broken –
  The joy o'th' moarning brasted afoor neet;
 Oh! faowl un feoful blow hed Deoth then strucken –
  'Twould touch'd grim Death hissel to sin that seet.

He bow'd his yed, as ower the bed he caur'd,
  Un cuss'd, un cuss'd his deed childt's ice cowd cheek;
 Un fra his een big drops o' wayter paured,
  Mecking the coarpse wi boiling tears to reek.

Billy hed sang, 'Aw want to be an angel,'
   When listening for the saond o daddy's feet;
  Un Billy'd goan to be a little angel,
    When whaom his daddy coom fra' wark ut neet.

Williffe Cunliam

Inscription

(In book, entitled 'The Hannahs,' presented to a niece.)

Burnley Gazette, May 21st 1864

'Tis uncle's gift, with uncle's prayers
   That these in these pages thou may'st find
Choice food for more matured years,
   And feel thy power o'er human kind;
Blest with each virtue that endears
   A woman to the noble mind.

When, onward borne by cycling years,
   Youth merges into womanhood.
Oh! may the fruit, thy life then bears,
   Be worthy of so fair a bud;
And ev'ry gift, and ev'ry grace,
   Unto life's purpose dutiful.
Give nobler beauties to thy face;
   And make thee good as beautiful.

Vice will the fairest thing defame;
   And rob the form of ev'ry grace –
Put royalty itself to shame –
   For vice would mar an angel's face –
Make lustreless the hero's name:
   And doth God's own stamp on man deface.

Poesy and Poverty

Burnley Gazette, May 28th 1864

'He would be a poet!' they said, with a sneering,
   Of a penny-a-liner, who stood in the street.
His doggerel verse dinning forth in our hearing,
   To catch an odd penny for something eat.

'He would be an author – he would be poet;
   And, look you, his genius has brought him to that;
Poets always are poor – I've seen it – I know it –
   Mark that seedy old coat, and that batter'd old hat.'

I took stock of his garb – with strings tied together –
   So shabby and worn-out at elbows and knees;
And the sleeves had been turned into enamell'd leather,
   By leaning on tables – by ink stains and grease;

And 'that hat' was a 'queer 'un' – dinged, batter'd and napless.
   Done up in brown crape, that, no doubt, once was black.
An unique 'old tile' – crowning owner so hapless –
   'Twould have suited some mimic, of 'Lord Lovell' knack.

Unvested and shirtless, I opine, was that bosom;
   Dirty choker and coat buttoned up to the chin;
And the end of his nose was a big ruddy blossom –
   An odorous floweret of brandy or gin.

Boots, bursting and soleless; what queer-looking figure;
   But what if the world was to blame for all that?
A truce to ironical, cynical rigour,
   Though droll looks the muse a 'shocking bad hat.'

Ah! perhaps the world's contumely and scorning,
   With 'more knocks than halfpence' – its 'hitting him hard,'
Had made him a driveller; – its cold, heartless spurning
   Had stifled a genius – blighted a bard.

And to drown all his cares he poured rum down his throttle;
   And became thus a 'rum-un' from drinking of rum –
Sought a 'freedom from care' in 'big-bellied bottle.'
   Till compelled jingling jargon for halfpence to hum.

So poets are poor, are they – 'cause you have seen it?
    Well – poverty's better than fool's brainless scalp;
Perhaps authorship's crime – there may be something in it –
    But if one can't help it, of course, it can't be help'd.

I believe you are right, now, I feel in my pocket.
    There's not many bright effigied yellow discs in't: –
Poor genius! Dame Fortune does slight it, and mock it,
    'Stead of rolling on't 'yellow-boys,' bright from the Mint.

But, if from my pen, when I in the ink dash it,
    The gold flowed like ink; and brought me some gain;
If each word was a note, and some banker would cash it,
    Then I'd soon bring me gold by a stroke of my pen.

But it's just like the things poets always are dreaming,
    They're not a whit richer, dream ever so fair;
They never get fat on hope's fitful gleaming –
    For poets can't live upon fancies and air.

Yet if poets are poor, well, what does it matter?
    Their musings are love – their dreamings are sweet;
Why, poets, like cooks, would be very much fatter,
    If poems, like pies, were good things to eat.

But they care not a straw if the world be made jolly,
    'Tis to make world happier, better they sing;
Let them paint up its virtue, and daub up its folly,
    If never a penny their song to them bring.

They weep with the mourner, they laugh with the merry,
    They tell too the dark tale of sorrow and wrong;
Of beauty and love – of scenes, bright and cheery;
    They warn, cheer, and teach a whole world with their song.

They throw o'er life's sombreness bright sunny gilding,
    And echoes of joy in the grieving heart's spring;
They are stars in the gleaming, with which life is filled in;
    Their songs with life, light and love, cheerily ring.

Ah! love so enchanting; ah! bliss so ecstatic;
    Ah! pleasures of poesy, – untold by the tongue;
In hall or in cellar, in palace or attic,
    Content is the poet, there's wealth in his song.

His joys they are purer, his pleasures are sweeter;
    The founts of his pathos more easily flow;
His love is more ardent, his passion runs deeper;
    And his rapture springs up with an intenser glow.

His griefs are more bitter, his sorrows are sadder,
    His woes are more keen, and more racking his pain,
Than the dull plodding world's – though the world deems him madder,
    More frenzied, insaner, than all other men.

Such bliss – so exquisite – if sorrows are tarter,
    'Tis worth all the throbbings – the anguish of pain;
For mountains of gold his muse he'd not barter,
    Nor were world upon world by the forfeit to gain.

Oh! give him a cot—a plain rustic cottage,
    In its mud walls with ivy and roses shut in,
Mossy banks, ivied walls, gnarl'd oaks, and plain pottage,
    Away from the city's distraction and din.

A home in the vale by a blue crested mountain,
    With woods, and with meadowland, crag, steep, and plain.
With umbrageous groves, and clear gushing fountain,
    To live and to love in rapturous strain.

And there by the mirrowy tree-skirted river;
    Or where runs the sward-belted, flower-fring'd stream,
Or where rock-vexed spray breaks in gurgling shiver;
    There let him chant ye his word-painted dream!

There with the heaven's blue concave above him;
    And the golden sheen peeping through branch-woven shade,
With each Heaven-taught warbler trilling forth love-hymn,
    The wing'd insects humming – the bird-song in glade.

There let him learn from their ungarbl'd hymnings,
    True poetic art – sweetest cadence of song.
And his soul melt away in the full golden gleamings,
    Till rich molten truth is the glow of tongue.

Chanting his theme in tunes world-entrancing,
    Till a world pause, enraptnr'd with bliss in their toil;
And the light of his song, with magical glancing,
    Springs flower-bells of joy from its base sterile soil.

Williffe Cunliam

'Aor Peggy's Courting!'
(By Peggy's Mother)

Burnley Gazette, June 4th 1864

Aor Peggy's put on her best bonnet,
    Un donn'd her i th' best things hu hed;
  For wenches at her age – Gigh yon it! –
    Hev but fellies un coorting i th' yed.

Hu's coorting, they sen, wi o' mason –
    Licker let it aloan, – that hu hed!
  But, naoh. lasses weant lissen to raison:
    Varry soon, aw expect, hu'll get wed.

'Time enough,' said her feyther, 'when thirty,
    To begin wi' o felly, un wed;
  Nought no war, if hu waits till hu's forty:
    Hu'll, then, hev moar sense in her yed.'

'But,' he sed to me, 'Lass, we wer youngish,
    When we took't in aor yeds to be wed!
  Un, afore it, time seemed rayther longish : –
    But hud better keep singul – hu hed!'

'Ther's no place like whom – wi' her mother!
    If hu stirs, lass, hu'll warsen;' he sed,
  Aw'm shure! hu'll ne'er find such another,
    Hu's better off, naoh, nur if wed!'

But its noa use us prating and croaking;
    We cohn't drive it aot uv her yed;
  Hu seys, 'Mother, naoh just gie ow'r talking,
    Yo kno', feyther un yo wonst wer' wed.'

Sleep

Burnley Gazette, June 11th 1864

Welcome comes the hour of rest –
Sweet the snowy pillow
When the aching heart and breast
With the boon of sleep is blest;
And the tired form, sore prest
By hard toil, woos sleep and rest –
Seeks to rest its jaded powers
In the night's oblivious hours:
Limbs, with weariness distrest,
On the couch stretch'd – head at rest
Nestling on the pillow.

Then the eyelids droop in sleep –
Close in happy dreaming;
And the powers of slumber, deep,
Softly o'er the senses creep,
While the unyoked soul doth leap,
Wing'd by balmy, – blissful sleep,
O'er abyss of 'time and space,'
To a new world – happier place –
Into Dreamland – climb its steep,
And gain into Heaven a peep.
Welcome, happy hours of sleep!

Williffe Cunliam

Maud Mary

Burnley Gazette, July 2nd 1864

Maud Mary – sweet fairy! –
Two lips, like a cherry,
Red cheeks, like twin roses,
And the prettiest of noses;
Brown eyes, and hair shiny,
In silken curls twiny;
A little tongue prattling: –
In childish talk tattling –
Now shouting, now singing,
In laughter now ringing;
Now jumping and skipping,
Then down the yard tripping,
Like a merry young fay,
Bounding, happy in play.
Thou makes my heart cheery,
My own little fairy,
My darling Maud Mary.

The Recluse

Burnley Gazette, July 9th 1864

There knelt the monk with his shaven crown,
Of coarse grey serge was his cowl and gown;
And he counted his beads with a heavy sigh; –
Worn was his visage, and sunk was his eye,
With sorrowful fight, long vigils at night,
From shadow of eve to dawning of light,
He had kept in his cell, while pondering o'er
His missal, or, chaunting his prayers before
The virgin's shrine – but – no peace for his soul:
His guilt was not covered with gown or with cowl.
Would – that his soul could be shaven as bare
Of sin, as his tonsur'd crown of hair! –
Would – that long years of penance could buy
A sinless light for that hopeless eye: –
That the tears he wept and the vigils he kept,
(While abbot and friars the long hours slept,)
Brought pardon and peace to his guilty soul,
But the sin on his soul was a deed most foul,
He might wear out his life in penance and prayer –
He might fast, till his bones protruded as bare
Through his shrivelled skin, and his limbs were as thin
As the skeleton form, which Sir Hugh, in his sin,
Had starved, immured deep in his castle keep;
And which tortur'd his soul and robbed him of sleep.
Sir Hugh had a bride like an angel fair,
With a bright blue eye, and soft flaxen hair –
Softer than dame or spinster e'er spun;
Cheeks, that were fairer, saw never a one,
With the blush of rose, – in maidenhood's prime,
And her speech was as sweet as a minstrel's rhyme.
He had sought her hand with a praising tongue; –
He had wood her heart with fair speech, long,
But the lady looked coldly his love-suit on –
Another, fair Isabel's heart had won –
Nor presents, nor threats, nor promise, nor prayer
Could win him the love of the lady fair,
And he swore, by the saints, 'he would humble her pride –
Would force her to love him – would have her as bride,
Despite earth or heaven – would change her cold look.'

Sir Hugh 'slight or scorn of no woman would brook.'
He forced her away from her father's old halls,
And laughed at their threats in his strong castle walls.
And the knight forced the priest, to make her his wife,
Then vowed if she lov'd not, to starve out her life,
And he shut in the dolefullest donjon there
The newly made bride, so tender and fair,
And he mockingly laughed at her tears and cry
With demon's heart, and a demon's eye,
And the demon, Sir Hugh, had starved out the life
Of fair Isabel, e'er she could love him as wife.
Then deep remorse for the deed so foul,
Seized on Sir Hugh, and weighed on his soul,
Like the massive walls of his donjon keep,
Crushing his soul, and murdering sleep.
He fled from his keep and his lofty halls,
And shut himself up in a cloister's walls,
Seeking in life of penance and prayer –
In wearying vigils and fastings there
To rid his unshriven soul of its sin:
Pardon and peace for his soul to win;
But never a day in that cloister dim,
Brought ray of comfort to him.
A shrivelled shadow haunted him there,
At matins, at vespers – knelt by him in prayer,
Mocking his prayers, as he mocked in life,
The tears and prayers of his murdered wife.
Peace or rest never may come to his soul,
Peace or rest never for murder so foul –
Would that his guilt could die with his breath,
Bringing him pardon and peace with his death.

Benediction!

Burnley Gazette, July 18th 1864

Angels of beauty! Keep watch o'er her bed ;
Angels of love! guard from dangers her head;
Waft heaven's fragrance around in her sleep,
And her slumbers unbroken your lullabys keep,
   Of sweet Nona Nomino.

Breathe heaven's music around her, ye fair,
And whisper my love in her slumbering ear;
Roses and flowers strew to pillow her rest,
With no thorn left to pierce the innocent breast
   Of sweet Nona Nomino.

Brighten her hours with love's happiest beams;
Scatter ye pearls o'er the path of her dreams;
Twine golden strands in the thread her life;
And pure be the heart-joys, as maiden – as wife,
   Of sweet Nona Nomino.

Dark shades of trouble ne'er sadden her brow,
Nor grief's pallor spread o'er her cheek's modest glow;
Hot tears of anguish ne'er dim her bright eye;
Nor the cares of the world to the soul cause a sigh
   Of sweet Nona Nomino.

Blest be her life-lot wherever she goes,
And stainless and pure as the fresh fallen snows:
As guileless and pure – as pure now thou art;
And thy friends be as true as the love of thy heart,
   Sweet Nona Nomino.

Williffe Cunliam

Home Longings

Burnley Gazette, August 27th 1864

Home of the wanderer in wilds dark and dreary,
　　Sweet vale of Eden that never knows night –
Hope of the prodigal famished and weary,
　　When will thy meads bless the pining one's sight?

Fondly the exiled one's heart, ever mourning
　　For thy fair rivers and bright sunny skies –
To thy sweet gardens and balmy air turning,
　　For thy pure pleasures and ceaseless bliss, sighs.

Longingly gazes he o'er the dark river,
　　Straining his vision to catch a dim sight
Through the o'erhanging mists, but no mortal sight ever
　　May gain faintest glimpse of the regions of light.

Gladly he'd plunge into Death's surging torrent –
　　Would breast the dark river to reach the bright plains.
And there fling his soul in the crystal joy current,
　　And drown in its pleasures his toilings and pains.

Oh! for its music, its seraph-tongued hymnings,
　　The pure snowy robe, like the day's pearly light –
star-studded crown, like the sun's brightest gleaming,
　　feast of increasing, eternal delight.

Tear-Drops

Burnley Gazette, June 9th 1866

There are pangs and there are sorrows
    Far too deep for thought or word,
When depths of moanless anguish
    Cannot be conceived or heard.

When the face no grief sign beareth,
    Nor a shade of woe reveal,
May be acrid grief that teareth
    Ruthlesser than barbed steel!

When the eye betrays no feeling,
    Hidden 'neath the placid brow,
May be heart asunder riven
    With the bursting tide of woe!

As the mellow earth ne'er riveth
    'Neath the droppings of the shower;
And the welcome rain reviveth
    The with'ring sun-scorched flower.

So weeping grief allayeth,
    As dust in showers of rain;
And thus tears dissolve our sorrows,
    And leave not trace of pain.

Grief, the strongest manhood boweth;
    Melts the iron heart as snow!
And the soothing tear o'erfloweth,
    A sweet medicine for woe!

Good God in pity sendeth
    Liquid mercies for relief;
And the crystal tear-drop blendeth
    As an antidote for grief.

'Tis where the stream is shallowest,
    That the water rippleth most;
And where our woes are deepest,
    In the tide, are murmurings lost.

And the heart thats stricken – broken,
    May the bitterest woe-pangs feel,
Though no condensed grief – or token,
    From the secret fount up-well.

The Glance of Love

Burnley Gazette, June 16th 1866

Have ye felt the spell of the flashing eye,
   Beaming with angelic witchery,
The crimson flush of the tell-tale blush,
   Lit by the fire of sweet modesty;
When the tenderest thoughts of a guileless breast
   In the deepest depths of the soul recess'd,
By a waking consciousness is wrest
   From the secrecy of the guarding breast;
And the passion-tide, in an amorous flood,
   Rolls through the veins in the swelling blood,
Mounts from the heart to the blushing brow,
   Out-mirror'd there in a scarlet glow?

But one short glance, as a-hastening by,
   Teeming with angelic witchery!
A glance, and glow o'er the started brow,
   And the fair round cheek, as eye met eye:
A glance of such meaning as speech cannot tell,
   With tongueless eloquence seeming to swell,
And where fathomless depths of sweet mystery dwell;
   And our souls are enbound by the magic spell;
By the witching art of the wondrous love,
   Then no longer free, we laugh and rove
At the snarer's wiles, as in days agone,
   For the golden gyves of love are on!

Notes

'A Wedding Rhyme ...' (**p.1**) William Cunliffe's first publication in the *Burnley Free Press and General Advertiser* was a relatively conventional celebration of the recent marriage between the Prince of Wales, Edward, and the Danish Princess Alexandra, who eventually became King and Queen of the UK on Queen Victoria's death in 1901. The poem is patriotic in tone and uses expected military and imperial terms, but already Cunliam's distinctive control of rhythm is evident, and triple rhymes throughout show confidence.

'Labor Omnia Vincit' (**p.2**) This poem's Latin title translates as 'work conquers all', which is a direct quotation from Virgil's *Georgics*, suggesting the breadth of Cunliffe's reading. In its historical context, it can be seen as a direct response to the widespread unemployment and displacement caused by the Lancashire Cotton Famine 1861-65. Many workers were forced to take up unfamiliar modes of employment after cotton mills closed. There was widespread worry that a dispirited workforce would succumb to idleness and bad habits, and this is part of a trend in the region of poems encouraging the values of resilience and diligence.

'Praying George' (**p.3**) The first Lancashire dialect poem Cunliffe published in the *Burnley Free Press* is this extraordinary example of social observation, focussing on a local character, a street sweeper, who is celebrated for his simplicity and religious devotion. The phonetic spelling of Burnley speech patterns in the poem are quite consistent with Cunliffe's other works in the vernacular, with the distinctive Lancastrian 'ao' vowel which some other dialect writers spell 'eaw'. Unusually, one word is provided with a 'translation' – 'duds' is revealed to refer to 'cloathes'.

'Adieu!' (**p.5**) There is a biographical aspect to this poem because Cunliffe did leave 'lov'd England' for five years from 1853 when he lived in the US. The piece seems to be a memory of the emotions of leaving his home country, in a similar vein to another poem in this collection, 'Granny!'. The final two stanzas perhaps refer to more recent events, with tensions between the UK and the Union in the wake of the Trent Affair of 1861-62, or perhaps they look back to the Crimean War of 1853-55.

'Sweetheart Fair' (**p.6**) This playful, observant dialect poem describes scenes of young adults attending a fair after church on a Sunday and the associated flirting and parading. Quite apart from the social details included here, there are interesting references to the types of clothing worn by the subjects (silks, cottons, merinos, paper collars, shiny beavers, peg-top breeches, and patent pumps), and real Burnley locations such as 'th' Bull nook' and 'Roberts-row', which was a row of terraced houses which once stood on the town's Manchester Road.

'Weighing the Anchor' (p.8) Cunliffe's poetic range is on display here as he attempts a sea shanty, complete with a 'heave, oh' refrain. Again, the poem uses triple rhymes to build tension before the repeated exclamations and although it is fairly light on nautical terms, it still reads as though it comes from someone familiar with sea voyages. Whether this is a memory from the poet's long journey across the Atlantic ten years before, or a poem which was written during that time, we may never know.

'Th' Petched Shirt' (p.10) Along with sterling historical detective work from staff at Burnley Central Library, this poem helped to identify 'Williffe Cunliam' as William Cunliffe, with the first line's reference to a 'smithy' (blacksmith's workshop) corroborating the poet's daytime profession (another Burnley 'William Cunliffe' was a 'wool sorter'). The poem itself compares favourably with similar examples of dialect social observation from Rochdale's Edwin Waugh, or Blackburn's William Billington. The message of the piece is also relevant to the contemporary poverty associated with the Cotton Famine, with one character chiding the other for being snobbish about mended clothing hanging on a washing line.

'Strike While the Iron is Hot' (p.12) While this poem's message appears to be the kind of generalised self-help advice associated in the Victorian era with writers such as Samuel Smiles (1812-1904), its references to blacksmith work in its metaphor can obviously be connected biographically with its author. It is one of several poems that Cunliffe wrote which celebrate the virtues of fortitude, courage, and diligence, and can be read in the context of the unstable employment situation in Burnley during the Cotton Famine crisis.

'Hoamly Chat' (p.13) This dialect poem concerns the issues of the Cotton Famine directly and takes the form of a conversation between two Burnley residents on the street. They discuss the dire economic situation including 'half-time' and unemployment, and associated poverty. The poem pointedly ends with one of the speakers blessing those who contribute to aid for stricken workers. An extract of this piece was published in the *Times* in November 2016, when media interest in the emerging Cotton Famine poetry project was at its height. The editor of this volume provided a 'translation', even though such explanations were apparently not required by London residents who read Lancashire dialect poems in the 1860s.

'Vanitas!' (p.15) Like two other poems in this collection, this poem's title is in Latin. In this case the term translates as 'vanity', but in the sense of a vain pursuit. It is another piece which might be read in a biographical context, as the speaker seems to be searching for meaning in life and engages first with poetry, then with the sciences, before finally finding satisfaction and fulfilment with religious devotion. With references to 'ignis-fatuus' ('will-o-the-wisp phosphorescent marsh lights), alchemy, and philosophy, there is more evidence of Cunliffe's depth of reading and appreciation of the wider themes of Victorian poetry.

'Congratulation' (p.17) Like the first poem in this collection this is a verse which celebrates a wedding. However, rather than a royal event, the happy couple are not identified here, and the poem is specifically addressed to the bride, suggesting that it might be intended for a relative of the author. It is not poetically distinctive in any real way, but it does showcase Cunliffe's characteristically confident sense of rhythm and metre.

'Misgivings!' (p.18) The speaker of this piece appears to be an abandoned lover, or at least one who fears abandonment at the outset of a journey. This kind of generalised and sentimental verse was commonly published in newspapers in the Victorian period, and in this case the poetic speaker is quite dramatic and self-pitying in their diction. In a narrative sense, the poem works as a snapshot of particular moment in a relationship.

'The Daisy' (p.19) This poem begins as a post-Romantic celebration of the beauties of nature, and particularly the ways that nature connects with human emotion. After the first stanza's descriptive passages the second uses the daisy as an 'aide memoire', suggesting that it sets off a train of childhood memories of play and innocence. By the third stanza the flower has become a symbol of simplicity and resilience, teaching the speaker to make the best of all situations in life. The final stanza progresses this moral element into a spiritual analogy, with the red petal tips apparently representing the blood of martyred saints. However, like much of Cunliffe's religious references in his poetry, and in keeping with a broad newspaper readership, there is enough linguistic vagueness that various Christian denominations might appreciate the sentiment.

'Settling th' War' (p.20) 'Settling th' War' is a humorous, ironic poem giving political satire a local flavour. It is William Cunliffe's most well-known poem, which after it was 'discovered' in 2015 featured in publications such as the *Guardian* and the *Sunday Times*; it has also been quoted in various BBC radio programmes. The dialect form used here is quite dense, but part of the reason for this is to show how incongruous it is that Burnley bigwigs, arguing on the streets of the town, think they can have any effect on an event as international as the American Civil War. Interestingly, in contrast to some popular views which like to remember Lancashire people in almost total sympathy with the Union cause, in the penultimate stanza the poem has Burnley residents apparently evenly split between support for Jefferson Davis (Confederate) or Abraham Lincoln (Union).

'God Help the Poor' (p.22) There are many Victorian poems with this title, including a famous one by Samuel Bamford (1788-1872) which was quoted in Elizabeth Gaskell's 1848 novel, *Mary Barton*. This poem by Cunliffe was quoted in the *Smithsonian Magazine* in 2018 when it picked up on the discovery of the hundreds of poems which led to the creation of the Cotton Famine poetry database. It updates the title's sentiment to make it more relevant to the contemporary economic crisis, especially by calling for peace in the American Civil War (which would lead to the re-opening of cotton mills). If anything, Cunliffe makes his poem less religious than other versions, and there is more emphasis on a call for genuine acts of charity which would save lives during a period of extreme poverty for millions of people.

'Thenkful Jone' (p.24) This dialect poem is another which directly references the American Civil War as the cause of local unemployment and poverty, and it is in the voice of the matriarch of the title. The family meal is described as being without meat, but the diners declare that they are happy with their lot and in such good heart that dry porridge tastes like roast beef. There is an interesting reference to the 'bacon' that the family receives from the local relief committee, and this is corroborated by other poems from the period which suggest that often this cheap meat was the only one available to poverty-stricken families. Jone's piety at the end of the poem becomes a complete acceptance of the situation, and it is likely that poems such as this functioned to advertise the moral uprightness of the working classes in order to justify continuing relief and charity.

'The Little Star Gazer' (p.25) This is one of several Cunliffe poems which celebrates the innocence of childhood, and in this the author is in good company, with hundreds of Victorian writers projecting their ideas and morality onto infants and children. Here, the speaker watches their young child staring at the night sky and imagines what they consider the stars to be or mean. The poem becomes progressively more religious in its language until the idea emerges that the child imagines the stars to represent the eventual resting place of dead children. Infant mortality rates were so high in the nineteenth century that this was a common subject in literature. However, the particular idea of children almost literally 'ascending to heaven' in this way may have been inspired by Charles Dickens' 1836 short story 'A Child's Dream of a Star'.

'Sham Abrum' (**p.26**) In his short literary career, William Cunliffe appears to have attempted almost all contemporary poetic forms, and here he offers an elegy in dialect. There is perhaps a political angle at the beginning of the piece when it is noted that poor people are often not remembered when they die in contrast to 'big foaks'. This skilful poem redresses that balance by paying homage to the life of a man whose devotion to his disabled wife was widely appreciated by the community. Like 'Praying George' in a previous dialect poem, 'Sham Abram' appears to have been a street sweeper, and there is a wonderful analogy in the final stanza of personified 'Deoth' sweeping all souls away, 'good, bad, un all.' 'Besom' is an archaic term for a broom which dates from at least Tudor times.

'Love!' (**p.28**) As quite a conventional celebration of romantic love in the most generalised terms, this is one of the least accomplished or distinctive poems in the collection. Even the metre is unremarkable, with eight- and seven-syllable alternating lines appearing like a trochaic ballad form. Like many Cunliffe poems, a seemingly secular subject is given a spiritual twist towards the end, with a vague conception of heaven representing a place where all lovers will be reacquainted.

'Come Bob, We've tu Markit i'th' Taon' (**p.29**) This dialect conversation between a man and his wife can be seen almost as a companion piece to Edwin Waugh's celebrated 'Come Whoam to thi' Childer and Me' from 1856. Waugh's poem, which also reconciled a difference between a married working-class couple, was nationally famous the decade before, and Cunliffe's poem similarly shows domestic tensions smoothed as the man relents and accepts domestic responsibility. In the Victorian period the term 'petticoat' was occasionally used as a synecdoche for feminine power (H. Rider Haggard dismisses this item of clothing at the beginning of his 'boy's own' adventure *King Solomon's Mines*), and initially Bob complains that his life is 'pettycoyt-led'. There is an interesting use of the dialect term 'druffen' here, meaning 'drunk'. Like 'gradely', 'threopin', and 'clem', 'druffen' appears to be of Nordic/Germanic origin, and even now there is a slang German term 'druff' which means high (on drugs).

'Despondency' (**p.31**) Romantic poets such as Samuel Taylor Coleridge, Keats, and Percy Shelley popularised poetry exploring the complexities of human emotion, and this literary tradition continued into the Victorian period. Here, Cunliffe uses deliberately archaic language such as '-eth' endings for verbs not just as poetic conventions, but to lend the poem a universal register. The reference to Gilead at the end of the poem uses the biblical placename as a desired destination metaphor.

'Work, Lads, and Think' (**p.32**) Labour poems such as this were common throughout the Victorian period in publications likely to be read by working-class audiences, but they were especially prevalent in Lancashire during the Cotton Famine. Like in 'Labor Omnia Vincit', the anxiety behind this poem seems to be that a disrupted workforce loses it industrious habits and idleness becomes endemic. With no proper names or places referenced, the poem appears universal in its message, but the mention of 'praise ... from the heart of a nation' (l. 19) might refer to the national scrutiny that the region was under during the Cotton Famine. Lancashire workers were widely praised for their positive response to the crisis, with even the Chancellor of the Exchequer, William Gladstone, suggesting that their behaviour merited eventual political representation. It was 1867 before the first working-class men achieved the vote in the UK.

'Sundey 'T Moarning' (p.33) This cheerful, positive dialect poem contains a wealth of domestic detail in its description of a family's Sunday morning ritual around breakfast. Strikingly, the second of the octet stanzas is devoted to the cleanliness of the abode, which, in lieu of expensive material goods was long an important marker of working-class value and status. It might be that 'Tum' (Tom), who does the cooking, is the eldest brother, but if so, no other adults are mentioned in the piece. The penultimate line appears at first confusing with reference to both a road and a street ('daon th' street o'th roayd to th' school'), but in this case 'roayd' is used in the northern English sense to mean 'way'. There is some clever word play throughout the poem, but a standout example is when 'flourish' becomes 'florridge' to rhyme with 'porridge'.

'Granny!' (p.35) Although concocted sentimental family poems such as this abound in Victorian literature, there are strong indications that this piece is autobiographical, with the memories of a beloved grandmother representing real experience. Cunliffe did travel to America as a young man in the mid-1850s, and may well have returned to find his grandmother had died in his absence.

'Owd Jinny's Egsperianze' (p.36) This poem in the voice of an octogenarian woman is composed in quite dense dialect that may reflect the more archaic speech patterns of its older character. To put it into context this character would probably have been born in the 1780s. The verse is melancholy in register, with 'Jinny' ruing the fact that she has lived so long, and apparently only remembering the misery she has witnessed in her long life. As a male writer, Cunliffe seems more willing than most to assume female voices in his poetry, and the plight of working-class women is rarely far from his poetry in standard English or dialect. The fifth stanza of this poem in particular details the downfall of once-happy young women with poverty, alcoholism, and unemployment amongst the social issues referenced.

'Frost-Work' (as 'Williffe Cunliffe') (p.37) This is one of two works in the collection where Cunliffe almost publishes under his real name, with 'Cunliffe' substituted for the customary 'Cunliam'. I suspect that both of these cases represent errors by the poetry editor, as there seems no reason why these poems in particular should give more of a clue to their author than any others. In a small town like Burnley, where Cunliffe was quite a well-known figure and spoke at local meetings, it is unlikely that his pen name was much of a disguise anyway. This poem, like its subject, is a delicate, ephemeral piece. It showcases its author's control of imagery, and may indirectly allude to Samuel Taylor Coleridge's 1798 conversation poem, 'Frost at Midnight'.

'Our Darling' (as 'Williffe Cunliffe') (p.38) The second poem attributed to 'Williffe Cunliffe' is another poem which celebrates the innocence of childhood, although in this case the description seems intensely personal. In fact, Cunliffe did not marry and have children until at least six years after this, so the inspiration for this and other child poems in the collection most likely came from the children of his siblings. Indeed, 'Inscription' reveals itself to be addressed to the speaker's niece. Although these poems might be read and appreciated by any parents reading them in their local newspaper, they might also have been composed on behalf of, or dedicated to, family members.

'A Humble Tale' (p.39) The 'humble' in 'A Humble Tale' is really a class description, with the narrative concerning the lives of two 'maiden-sisters' and their tribulations. As in several Cunliffe poems, the plight of working-class women is to the fore and themes of domestic duty superseding personal happiness are prevalent. Like the poem 'Sham Abram' there is a disabled female character who requires lifelong care, which in this case prevents her sister from marrying. The ending is typical of Victorian melodrama, with a badly wounded returning soldier requiring the care of the surviving sister until they are briefly married and both die.

'Hora Fugit!' (p.41) 'Hora Fugit!' (time flies) is another Cunliffe poem with a Latin title, and like the others it is abstract and broadly philosophical in nature. In this case the subject is the transient nature of life, but there appears to be no moral or message in the poem – it simply emphasises the ineffability of death. Nor indeed is there any trace of Cunliffe's Christian faith in relation to the subject of mortality, which is a little odd. Although this was published in the January of 1864, it is known that Cunliffe's mother died later that year. It may be that she was ailing already, and this was an expression of a young man (he was thirty-one) facing up to the inevitable loss of his mother.

'A Rhyme for the Time' (**p.42**) There are many Victorian poems with this title, or titles very like it, and in this case the real subject is the Lancashire Cotton Famine. In a narrower sense it belongs to a class of poems which urged working-class readers to keep faith that the economic situation would eventually improve, and that fuller employment and higher wages would return. Although the anxiety of social unrest is usually implicit in these poems Cunliffe addresses the potential full on with the line 'Go not trouble-seeking, friends' (l.21). In fact, given the extent of economic deprivation and poverty, the Cotton Famine saw very little 'trouble', and the end of the American Civil War the year after this poem was published saw the return of cotton to the mills and generally improved social conditions.

'The Lass o' Pennul Waytur' (**p.43**) As is sometimes the case with texts from 160-year-old newspapers, the existing copies of 'The Lass 'o Pennul Waytur' were almost illegible, but with thanks for the assistance of staff at Burnley Central Library, we were eventually able to make a complete transcription of this wonderful dialect song. I describe it as a song because its repeated refrain and bouncing rhythm place it in a class alongside traditional English ballads. If Cunliffe did compose this independently of existing folk ballads, then it shows a remarkable grasp of the form, complete with references to real local place names, with some like 'Gawthrup' (Gawthorpe) and 'Taonley' (Towneley Park), and the titular 'Pennul Waytur' (Pendle Water) rendered in dialect versions. This is yet another piece which displays Cunliffe's impressive poetic versatility, even within the dialect form. Incidentally, it is also the first piece that Cunliffe publishes in the newly established *Burnley Gazette*, having previously published in the *Burnley Free Press and General Advertiser*. In reality this is a name change rather than a new publication, as one newspaper took over the function of the other.

'The Angel of My Home' (**p.44**) While this is another of Cunliffe's poems which celebrates the charm and innocence of children, there is something interesting about the title he chooses. In 1854 the poet Coventry Patmore (1823-96) published the first of many editions of a long poem called *The Angel in the House*. This became very famous/infamous as a male-centred view of female domestic roles, and even in its own time some critics saw it as part of a developing trend which placed social limits on the activities of women, particularly in terms of the freedom to undertake paid work. This trend was less prevalent in northern working-class communities, where the largest working demographic in cotton mills tended to be adult females. Here, Cunliffe plays on Patmore's title and has the 'angel' as the child, pointedly referring to '*My* Home' as though to resist Patmore's infantilisation of women. Nobody could describe Cunliffe as a feminist, but his treatment of women in his poetry at the very least highlights the difference between culturally prevalent middle-class views of the roles of women and the reality of life for working people in industrial areas.

'Guilty, My Lord!' (p.45) The theme of this poem is religious penitence, and the speaker addresses the divine with regret for earthly sins. The language is metaphor-heavy and hyperbolic, and there is an emphasis on mercy and the unworthiness of the speaker. In keeping with other religious poems that Cunliffe published in the *Free Press* and the *Gazette*, biblical references and specific religious practices are kept to a minimum, which allows the poem to operate across various religious denominations. Burnley, like most Lancashire towns, contained a mix of religious establishments and practices, with Roman Catholics, Anglicans, and Nonconformists of various hue all co-existing.

'Heaven!' (p.46) This short poem, like the previous religiously themed piece, is quite general in its expression of religious faith. Its topic is the unknowable nature of paradise in the afterlife. There is an interesting element in the recognition of the failure of not just imagination to guess at the nature of heaven, but language to describe it. Like in the earlier 'Vanitas!' there is a preference for religious devotion over 'poesy', taken to refer to the consideration of, or writing of, poetry.

'Leather-Yed Tay' (p.47) One of the poets who was often published alongside 'Williffe Cunliam' in the poetry columns of Burnley newspapers was 'S. Holden', who occasionally offered verse which promoted the Temperance message. Temperance, the encouragement of abstinence from, or at the very least moderation of, alcohol intake, was associated with some Nonconformist organisations. The Temperance movement was given a considerable boost during the Cotton Famine, when the moral worth of the working classes was under particular scrutiny. 'Leather Head Tea' was an ironic term for a drink which purported to be 'soft' but in fact contained alcohol. The comic treatment of the drunkenness of the character 'Jimmy Joyful' in this humorous dialect poem suggests that, whatever Cunliffe's religious leanings, he was not overly earnest in his consideration of Temperance issues.

'Not for Ourselves Alone' (p.48) This poem, which begins with very extensive use of the poetic device of 'anaphora' – the repetition of the first words of lines, appears at first to celebrate the interconnectedness of nature. However, along with increased references to the divine as the poem progresses, the final stanza reveals the true theme of the piece to be charity, which places it within the context of the Lancashire Cotton Famine. The spirit of community is presented first as naturally universal, but then is narrowed until the last line addresses the reader directly and suggests that only the individual can embody God's role as a donor ('almoner').

'Nellie's Grave' (p.49) Like 'A Humble Tale', this piece represents a longer, narrative poem. In this case, however, the narrator appears as a character at the beginning of the poem, and the story itself is recounted through a conversation with an old sexton. Although the narrative has a fairytale quality to it, with the mysterious young woman appearing in a village and the rustic description, in reality this poem can be considered alongside the work of famous contemporary poets including Christina Rossetti, in that it appears to subtly refer, without moral judgement, to issues of single motherhood. Given that a baby is buried alongside Nellie when she dies, there is a possibility that she died in childbirth, and was pregnant when she arrived in the community. Nevertheless, it is pointedly noted that she is 'lov'd by ev'ry one', indicating social acceptance. Nellie does not reveal her 'wrongs', despite the attempts of 'gossips', she is not referred to as a widow, and the sexton, representing the religious establishment, does not pass judgement.

'**The Evening Bell**' (p.52) This is the first of three bell poems that Cunliffe published in the spring of 1864. It is composed of four-line quatrains in 'ballad metre', where four-beat lines alternate with three-beat lines. This gives the verse a songlike rhythm, and the sound of the church bells is depicted as having a soothing effect on the speaker, as much for their regularity as for their status as marking time or serving as a call to prayer. There is a theme of passing time throughout the piece, with a particular emphasis on the transition from youth to manhood, and subsequent decline. It is worth remembering that Cunliffe was still in his early thirties when he wrote these poems. He seems to be writing on behalf of other characters (or perhaps representing the concerns of family members), or projecting into his own later life.

'**The Sabbath Bells**' (p.54) This second bell poem is very different from the first. In tonal register it is joyous, focussing on church bells as a call to prayer which leads to individual salvation and communal support. It is also quite experimental in structure, with the careful indentation of the lines echoing the rhythmic chime of church bells. This effect is compounded by the use of short lines of three or four syllables, and the occasional use of triple rhymes (forth/earth/north; towers/bowers/flowers) which mimic the repetition of bells ringing. Although the poem appears to address the sabbath bells at the beginning, it embodies them later, especially in the multiple repetition of lines beginning 'Come ... ', where various types of worshippers are called to prayer. The poems final lines cleverly compress six '-ung/-ong' rhymes – those which sound most like bells.

'**The Passing Bell**' (p.56) As the third and final bell poem 'The Passing Bell' is different again from its predecessors. In its word choice and register it leans towards gothic literature, and indeed with its reference to 'Hades' and dark imagery, it does not really read as a religious poem; or not

Christian, in any case. Like 'The Sabbath Bells' it utilises short, indented lines to mimic the bell sound, and multiple rhymes to echo the chimes. Terms such as 'ghostly', 'groans', 'horror', and 'mould'ring' suggest the influence, perhaps indirectly, of Edgar Allan Poe, and reflecting that writer's morbidity a 'passing bell' is a bell rung immediately after a death in order to call congregations to prayer. However, prayer is not mentioned in the poem, and the bells instead are personified as a 'mocking demon' when their sound is distorted by the wind.

'Spring Time' (p.58) This quite conventional poem celebrates spring's abundance and its rejuvenating effect on nature and humanity. The first line is used as a refrain throughout the poem, beginning and closing every stanza, and this increases the songlike effect of the very regular metre and rhyming couplets between the refrains. As in so many Cunliffe poems of this period, there is an emphasis on themes of redemption and recovery, but here it is nature rather than religious engagement which provides the key. One interesting phrase with a slight ecclesiastical tone is 'feathr'd chorists', to mean 'songbirds'. This is an example of what is known in rhetoric as 'periphrasis' (literally 'writing around'), a poetic effect of indirect speech used particularly by the earlier generation of Romantic poets. For example, in Wordsworth's 'The Female Vagrant' (1798) a character refers to a flock of sheep as a 'fleecy store'.

'The Stolen Bud' (p.59) This is another example of a poem where Cunliffe uses distinctive indentation to give the poem shape on the page and to indicate pauses in different places. Although some of the imagery in the piece echoes the sensual language of Christina Rossetti ('The Goblin Market' was published two years before this), the bud appears to be a metaphor for a deceased child or infant. If this is an elegy for a family member or a child whose parents Cunliffe knew, then it unusually subtle, because the real subject is never explicitly revealed. However, the final image of the bud blooming 'immortally' strongly suggests that the topic of this poem is infant mortality, and when that tragic phenomenon reached unprecedented heights during the Cotton Famine, this poem may have been a comfort to many grieving readers in the Burnley area.

'Sunshine' (p.61) This poem, written in a Romantic mode, celebrates the power of the sun and is full of elaborate imagery relating to its functions and effects. Like several Cunliffe poems of this period it is composed with a complex indentation system utilising often very short lines which allow for an effect of listing, but also place emphasis on individual phrases. However, while many Romantic poems celebrate nature in secular or even quasi-pagan terms, this poem turns in its last stanza to reveal its subject as representative of the power of the divine, interestingly using the Old Testament term 'Jehovah'.

'Little Billy' (p.64) This moving dialect poem is on the subject of infant mortality, and while it does not attribute a cause to the child's death, it would have been especially poignant published in the mid-1860s when the Cotton Famine saw widespread poverty and hunger lead to an increase in mortality rates. Although poets such as Joseph Ramsbottom (Manchester), Samuel Laycock (Ashton-Under-Lyne), and William Billington (Balckburn) wrote dialect poetry accounts of the effects of the Cotton Famine, it is rare for this vernacular mode to treat a dark subject in such an individual way. Cunliffe appears to be incorporating a strong degree of social observation into his verse, and to be highlighting the human cost of economic hardship. It is worth noting that during this period many people employed in Billy's father's profession, cotton weaving, saw their wages cut due to the importation of substandard cotton and reduced working hours.

'Inscription' (p.66) This poem claims to be, and probably was, intended as an inscription in a book given as a gift to the writer's niece. Cunliffe was the youngest of several siblings so it is highly likely that he would have had nieces or nephews at reading age during this period of his life. Perhaps a modern equivalent to this poem is Philip Larkin's 'Born Yesterday' (1954), written for Kingsley Amis's daughter, Sally. That poem wishes ordinariness on its addressee to avoid a lack of balance in life, and Cunliffe similarly hopes that duty and grace will make their mark on his niece's face as much as beauty. There appears to be a real thought for the future of the child here, but a paternalistic moralising takes over in the last stanza, which becomes fixated on 'vice'. The 1860s saw a moral panic over sexual behaviour, leading to legislation against sexually transmitted diseases, and broader cultural campaigns encouraging further social regulation of the behaviour of women.

'Poesy and Poverty' (p.67) This fascinating poem in quatrains with alternating rhymes discusses the relationship between poetry and the material world. It begins by resisting the mockery of an impoverished poet figure, but then develops into something like a call for funding for the arts (!), and a justification for poets as vital parts of a functioning society. The poet figure at the beginning is described as a 'penny-a-liner', which relates to the ancient tradition, especially in Lancashire towns, of selling printed ballads on the street for a penny a time. However, in this case, the poet performs the poem to a group for a penny, and the crux of the poem is whether, even if the poem is 'doggerel', this practice amounts to begging. The speaker describes the tattered, dishevelled appearance of the poet, and the fact that he is most likely an alcoholic, but nevertheless celebrates his talents, and calls for society to financially support him and his kind.

'Aor Peggy's Courting!' (p.70) As far as we know this is the last dialect poem that Cunliffe published. It is a relatively light-hearted piece, and it purports to be spoken by a young woman's mother, discussing the possibility of an impending marriage. In common with many dialect poems of the period – and with Cunliffe's own 'Come Bob ... ' – the basis of the poem is effectively a dialogue between man and wife. In this case the father is resistant to the idea of his daughter marrying, while conceding that he and his wife were courting when they were her age. At the end of the piece 'Peggy' makes the same point for herself and it seems the family is resigned to the nuptials. The poem is interesting in terms of class and gender, and the extent to which a young woman has control over her own destiny in matters such as this. In working-class households there was often the added issue that a woman of marrying age would also be working (often in the cotton mills), and that the marriage of a daughter would represent a significant drop in income for a family.

'Sleep' (p.71) While the topic and imagery in this poem are not especially unusual, Cunliffe typically uses poetic devices to mirror the subject in quite an innovative way. The use of multiple rhymes within stanzas (there are seven '-ests' in the first and eight '-eeps' in the second) is intended to have a repetitive, soporific effect, perhaps equivalent to the practice of 'counting sheep'. In the first stanza, no doubt drawn from Cunliffe's profession as a working blacksmith, the emphasis is on bodily fatigue, with references to 'hard toil', 'distrest' limbs, and a 'tired form'. The poem is a largely secular ode to the state of sleep, but it also suggests in its closing lines that sleep represents a brief view of 'Heaven'.

'Maud Mary' (p.72) This simple, light poem, like 'Our Darling' and 'the Angel of My Home' is seemingly a loving tribute by a father to his infant daughter. However, as previously noted, Cunliffe was childless at this point in his life and the poem may be intended for a friend or family member. The short lines and rhyming couplets give the piece the appearance of a song, and the language is largely fairytale-inspired. However, one domestic detail indicates the social class of the subjects: this 'fairy' or 'fay' does not play in a garden but in a 'yard', often the only outdoor domestic space available to working people living in terraced housing.

'The Recluse' (p.73) 'The Recluse' is an unusual piece for Cunliffe, in that it is a gothic narrative of some length, at least for a newspaper poem. It is written, as so many narrative poems were during the nineteenth century, in iambic pentametre rhyming couplets (sometimes known as 'heroic couplets'), and its lack of historical detail and reference to castles, and characters who are monks, knights, and maidens, suggests a timeframe of the Middle Ages. This is an example of the kind of 'Neo-medievalism' which more famous poets such as Christinna Rossetti, Robert Browning, and Alfred Lord Tennyson indulged in, and this was often a way that writers addressed contemporary themes through an historical narrative. The theme here is male control and violence, with the main character a nobleman who imprisons and starves a young woman to death when she refuses to sleep with him after having marriage forced upon her. The poem ends with the knight unsuccessfully seeking penance in his status as a monk, as he is haunted by the cries of his murdered wife.

'Benediction!' (p.75) Framed as a benediction, or well-wishing prayer, for a child or infant, this is effectively a lullaby, with the refrain of 'sweet Nona Nomino' lending the piece a songlike rhythm. 'Nona Nomino' literally translates from Latin as 'your name that is Nona', which perhaps suggests that 'Nona' is an affectionate nickname rather than a given name. Like the earlier 'Inscription' poem, this verse looks forward to a child's adulthood, and alongside good fortune wishes for moral uprightness. However, unlike 'Inscription' the moral element of the piece is kept to a minimum, and the poem is good-natured in its address.

'Home Longings' (p.76) This poem is composed in alternating rhymes in a dactylic three-footed metre, almost like a waltz or the sound of a horse's hooves. The theme of a wanderer returning home might seem to place the piece as one written several years before when Cunliffe returned from his long stay in the United States, but in fact the topic of homecoming appears to be a metaphor for the release of death. Eden and Heaven are conflated and presented as a return to origins for the soul. The rhythm is remarkably well controlled here, and Cunliffe changes the lineation in the last stanza, when the alternating indentation shifts to a kind of fading slope. The effect of this is to emphasise the transition of the soul of the subject into paradise.

'Tear-Drops' (p.77) In the latter part of the period in 1864 when William Cunliffe was publishing poetry in the *Burnley Gazette* as 'Williffe Cunliam' he was also, under the same pseudonym, writing humorous prose sketches for the paper, occasionally in dialect. On September 3rd 1864, a letter was published in the newspaper which, although written in jokey puns, accused 'Cunliam' of writing an account of a local association's excursion to the countryside without their permission. This transgression appears to have been taken seriously because Cunliffe's work disappeared from the newspaper altogether for nearly two years. He never wrote any more prose sketches under the 'Cunliam' pseudonym, and only two more poems appeared, both in the summer of 1866. 'Tear-Drops' was the first of these and for the most part it is a fairly unremarkable exercise in Victorian abstraction. The language is archaic and the imagery is relatively standard for this kind of poetry. Perhaps the standout element is the clever metaphorical adage contained in the penultimate stanza: ''Tis where the stream is shallowest, / That the water rippleth most'.

'The Glance of Love' (p.79) 'The Glance of Love' was the last poem that William Cunliffe published in the *Burnley Gazette,* and it is quite unusual in his body of work for its sensual, romantic subject matter. Its topic is relatively risqué – momentary erotic attraction, and while poems on this subject were written and published throughout the Victorian period, it is unique in Cunliffe's oeuvre, which more often treated sexuality in moral terms. In keeping with this poet's formal adventurousness, the rhyme scheme is unusual with the pattern of ABCBDDDDEEFF repeated for the second twelve-line stanza. The four D rhymes together build up tension in the middle of each stanza and there are repeated phrases and words throughout the piece which enhance the formal integrity. If this was the last poem that William Cunliffe ever published then it is not typical of his work, but then it would be difficult to identify a poem that was. This blacksmith-poet's work covered a wide range of subjects, styles, and forms, as the fifty-four poems in the collection prove.